The Great American
Sidewalk, Stoop, Dir[...]
Games

Also by the author:
The Great American Marble Book

THE GREAT AMERICAN BOOK OF SIDEWALK, STOOP, DIRT, CURB, AND ALLEY GAMES

by Fred Ferretti

Photographs by Jerry Darvin

Workman Publishing Company, New York

Library of Congress Cataloging in Publication Data

Ferretti, Fred.
   The great American book of sidewalk, stoop, dirt, curb, and alley
games.

   Includes index.
   SUMMARY: Describes the rules and equipment for a number of
age-old games still played today, such as dodge ball, jacks, marbles, curb
ball, and street checkers.
1. Games.   [1. Games]   I. Title.
GV1203.F37   790   75-7291
ISBN   0-911104-59-3

Cover design: Paul Hanson
Book Designer: Paul Hanson
Photographs: Jerry Darvin
Typeset by Innovative Graphics Inc.
Printed and bound by George Banta Company
Manufactured in the United States of America

PEPSI and PEPSI-COLA are Registered Trademarks of
PepsiCo, Inc.

Baseball cards courtesy of Topps Chewing Gum, Incorporated

Workman Publishing Company
1 West 39th Street
New York, New York 10018

First printing, September 1975

   3 4 5 6 7 8 9 10 11 12 13 14 15

This book is for Eileen, Christopher, Elena, and Stephen

For their letters, research, and good humor and for sharing their childhoods with me, I wish to thank the following gamespersons:

Richard Wanderer, Grace Ehrlein, Jeff Morley, Betsy Wade, Andy Fuchs, Elena Ferretti, William Weiss, Miriam Sarzin, Glenn Collins, Pat Wallace, Mike Kaufman, Sue Moyer, Joe Fried, Joel Skolnick, Anne Isenburger, Irving Perline, Al Cruz, Bruce Cisciotti, Marshall Schneider, Karl Gottesman, Abe Joel Smith, Clara Glasser, Bob McLean, George Morris, Stanley Marx, Francis Glimm, Abe Weiler, Alan Wagner, Jean Gard, Charles Ralston, Tuck Stadler, Mrs. Robert Rohdie, Mrs. G. MacManus, Alan Kahn, Vira Klawe, Paul Schreiber, Susan Revit, B. Hennessey, Sheila Migdon, Toby Shatzoff, L. J. Fischler, Beatrice Haskell, Albert Van Sauter, Aaron Rubin, Miriam Allen DeFord, Mrs. Leroy Fisher, Mark Goodman, Desiree Steiner, Arnold Levinson, A. Van Schyndel, William Newell, Alice Bertha Gomme, Morris Silverman, Joseph Gancher, Calvin Roth, Rhona Statland de Lopez, Harvey Grode, Michael Magnifico, Edmund Bosch, C. E. Meakin, Jean Parker, Lewis Bertrand, Paul Derian, Dorothy Kamen-Kaye, Harold Bialock, Marilyn Hennecken, Nicholas Hripcsak, Shelly Anderson, Iona and Peter Opie, Alice Winkler, Eva March Tappan

Johnny on a Pony—for strong backs and legs.

CONTENTS

In the corners for Four-Way Box Ball.

INTRO DUCTION

Down, down, down, baby,
Down by the rollercoaster.
Sweet, sweet baby,
I'll never let you go.

Shimmy shimmy coco pop
Shimmy shimmy pop
Shimmy shimmy coco pop
Shimmy shimmy pop.
Freeze!

JUST A LITTLE while ago, I was driving through Flushing, which is a part of Queens, which is a part of New York City; and for an unfathomable instant, I wondered about the block where I had grown up. Foolish wondering, too. I really did ask myself: Was it still there? Was my block still there? Well, of course it had to be, but what I was doing was what kids do all the time—believing that something which has been part of them just kind of vanishes if they're not there with it. Was the block the same? I certainly didn't know that. So, I detoured a few blocks and drove to Forty-third Road, and I found, in a flood of remembrances, that it looked very much the same as when I played Touch Football and Softball and Stickball with Kenny and Don and Janet, and Kick the Can with Eleanor (whom I liked) and Johnny, and cards with Charlie and Dotty and a bunch of other kids whose names I can no longer reach back and find.

Not much had been changed at all. The house in which I grew up and lived for twenty-four years looked about the same except that I didn't like the hurricane fence the present owner had encaged the house in. But the garage my father had built halfway up our alley—for the very good reason that his accumulation of urban junk treasures had filled up the other garage and there was no place for the car—was still there, and I liked that.

Actually, I shouldn't call what we had an alley. It was more in the nature of a driveway. On our block, the rows of houses across the street—the two family and three family—were separated by alleys. Single-family homes had driveways, thank you.

I drove around a bit, found that Feinstein's candy store—where I bought cigars for my father; milk for my mother; gum, ice cream, and Batman comics for myself; and nothing for my sister—had been replaced by a neighborhood branch bank. The tennis courts where I skulked about waiting to steal balls hit over the fence are gone, replaced by an apartment house. The empty lot where we built huts out of wood scraps and discarded refrigerator cartons, where we roasted "mickies," where in spring the weeds tasted sweetest, where in winter the snow stayed whitest longest, was filled with four new houses. "Mickies"—the right way to roast them was to dig a shallow hole in the dirt, line it with bricks, fill it with wood, start a fire, and drop the raw potatoes into the flames; they were cooked when their skins were reduced to jet-black powder. To my surprise, the basketball backboard we built and nailed to the telephone pole a couple of houses away from mine was still attached, although there was no hoop.

I found myself looking around for my friends, knowing they weren't there, but looking nevertheless. And I was not unhappy to find they were not there. The memories were almost as good.

I don't know if the path through the chest-high weeds behind the row houses is still there—it was at once a safari route, a French and Indian War trail, and a fine place for a guerrilla ambush—but I remembered exactly where it was. And the grocery store whose owner left just enough soda bottles out back so that we could take them and, with about four cents deposit each, get a daily ration of bubble gum and baseball cards. And I remember Eleanor's mother making sandwiches out of jelly doughnuts and ice cream that were the best on hot days, and the peashooter fights and all the ammunition one needed when the wild cherry trees bore small green pellets, and the showers made out of pipes and old shower heads and connected to hoses, and how good the ice off the back of the iceman's truck tasted in summer.

I remember winter, when all street games stopped and there was an afterschool rush to the golf course a mile away to sneak through holes in the fence so we could go sleighing. I remember Charlie, who liked to score Yankee games intricately as much as I did, and Willard, who was a Boy Scout when I wished I was one, and Coleman, whose father had a finished cellar that was filled with the exciting memories of twenty-five years in the navy and whose mother didn't mind preparing impromptu lunches for a dozen.

On my block, I won races, had the point of my nose sliced quite badly with the shards of a bottle and held together by my mother until the blood clotted because she didn't want stitches on my face, was excessively mean to my sister, and invented life. And when I was big, I moved away. That's what I thought about when I stopped in front of what used to be my house.

I only stayed on the block for a little while, and then I drove away to where I was going. But it had been nice to look at my block.

Children, particularly those in the suburbs, have mobility these days. They know the best coasting hills for bikes, the best flat places for Jump Rope, what playing fields are the most level for ball games. But there was a time when a youngster's out-of-the-house growing up was confined, except for school, to the block he happened to live on. The block—its gutter and sidewalks, stoops and empty lots—was known intimately; and children did not correct, or even attempt to correct, its flaws and cracks. Instead, with excellent accommodation, they created their play around them. An uprooted tree was a ground rule. There was another tree—it looked like all the other trees—that was everybody's back brace for Johnny on a Pony and one stoop off which, for some inexplicable reason, a spaldeen bounced best.

On the block, you knew who to avoid, which stoop belonged to a grouch,

which grown-ups would take and keep the ball if it landed over their hedge. There were cliques and clubs, hates and likes, feuds and deep friendships. The block was our universe, and on it, there was usually enough of everything for us. We were secure, insular. We thought, how could there be another block like ours?

But there were a lot of them.

A ball-hitting game was called Cat and Dog in Pittsburgh and One-O-Cat on our block, and our pig Latin was not unique, although we were sure it was. The kids in San Francisco Kicked the Can down those hills and also ate those wonderfully chilling shards of ice that the iceman gave out from the back of his truck. A batting game called Peggy in Boston was called Stick and Goose in England and Shchizhi in Moscow. Stickball in New York was Stickball in New Jersey and Cork Ball in Saint Louis, and Red Rover and Red Light, Green Light were American universals. Potato chips bought in a Puerto Rican grocery in New York's East Harlem tasted the same as those in Chicago. And once, there were no alternate-side-of-the-street parking restrictions in either place. Our block, it turns out, was a tile in a mosaic.

And we all played with the same things. Kids today have all manner of sports equipment, but we had thrown-out wood, broken roller skates, discarded carriage wheels, orange crate joints, and broomsticks, which we converted into basketball backboards, hockey nets, scooters and wagons, play guns, and bats. And we had our spaldeens.

A spaldeen—I sorrow that an explanation is necessary, but I have found out that there *are* people, *really*, who have never heard of, much less played with, a spaldeen. A spaldeen was—and is—a pink rubber ball, without fuzz, made by Spaulding. But nobody ever called it anything but a spal-*deen*.

When I was a kid, it cost ten, fifteen, twenty, twenty-nine, thirty-nine cents, maybe more, and was an all-purpose ball. There were imitations—the pennsy and the pinky, the British bouncer—which one resorted to in times of hardship, but no game played on the block was ever spiritually correct unless a spaldeen was used. That's just the way it was.

Some games were created on the block, others adapted to its geography. Rhymes were made up that were recognizable doggerel; yet, there were others, inexplicable to kids on another block, that suited one block just fine. There would be no problem, for example, with:

> *My mother gave me fifty cents*
> *To see the elephant jump the fence.*
> *He jumped so high*
> *He reached the sky*
> *And didn't come down till the Fourth of July.*

but what about:

> *Bobo skiwotten totten*
> *Eh eh*
> *Eh-eh boom-boom-boom.*
> *Bobo skiwotten totten*
> *Eh eh*
> *Eh-eh boom-boom-boom.*
> *Iddy diddy wotten totten*
> *Bobo skiwotten totten*
> *Eh eh*

Eh-eh boom-boom-boom.
Freeze!

To the first rhyme, you bounced a ball; to the second, you clapped. Clear?

Rhymes were necessities, and rules were important, even though they might change daily. Yesterday, two strikes was out; today, three. Why? Because yesterday was yesterday and today is today. A measure of block status was to be chosen captain for a team game, an honor usually conferred on the best player. And it was the captain who chose his team and occasionally dictated rule changes.

WHO GOES FIRST?

Before playing *any* game, it is necessary to decide who should go first. In virtually every game, going first carries a decided advantage. And how is it decided who goes first? If there are two boys, say, and one is much larger than the other, then there really isn't much of a problem. Larger and fiercer people always go first. But in a moderately democratic group, the simplest method is to choose with the fingers. If there are two players, a simple odds-and-evens game, in which you put out either one or two fingers, is just fine. With three or more, it is usually the odd finger who goes first. For example, if three players put out (at the count of 'One, two, three, *shoot!*") one finger each and a forth sticks out two, then the fourth gets to go first. But these choosings are for the impatient.

More often, elaborate rituals, with elaborate rhymes, are employed, which makes for a certain suspense and pregame spice that are almost as important as the games themselves. There are simple ones in which players stand in a circle, and the designated counter points at each player in turn, including himself, as he chants:

Eeny meeny miney mo,
Catch a tiger by the toe.
If he hollers, let him go.
My mother says to pick this one right
over here

19

Odds, evens. Who goes first?

And finger points. A more elaborate version, native to New Jersey, goes like this:

> *Eeny meeny disaleeny ooh*
> *Ah combaleeny coomaracha I love you.*
> *Take a peach, take a plum*
> *Take a piece of bubble gum.*
> *Dontcha like it?*
> *Dontcha take it.*
> *Do the Alabama shakeit.*
> *Shake it up, shake it down,*
> *Shake it all around the town,*
> *And out you go*
> *With a dirty dirty dishtowel*
> *Around your dirty toe.*
> *Not because you're dirty.*
> *Not because you're clean.*
> *Just because you kissed the girl*
> *Behind the magazine.*

The suspense with this is incredible, with the unwary newcomer believing that with the word *you* he has won, or to use another term, has been "duked," but realizing later that the word magazine, is at the moment of truth. Others are simpler and more direct:

> *Mickey Mouse built a house.*
> *How many bricks did he use?*

Five.
F-I-V-E spells five
And out you go.

or:

My mother and your mother
Were hanging up clothes.
My mother punched your mother
Right in the nose.
What color blood came out?
Purple.
P-U-R-P-L-E spells purple
And out you go. Now go!

or:

Engine, engine number nine
Going down Chicago line.
If the train goes off the track,
Do you want your money back?
No.
N-O spells no, *and out you go!*

or:

Sally over the ocean.
Sally over the sea.
Sally broke a bottle, and she blamed it all on me.

I told ma, ma told pa.
Sally got a spanking and a ha ha ha.

or:

Ibbity bibbity sibbity sah
Ibbity bibbity cannabo
Here or where crown a cat
Allaga Zallaga zo

In a Brooklyn version of another universal standard, players are not pointed at, but their hands are batted down as the counter says:

One potato, two potato,
Three potato, four.
Five potato, six potato,
Seven potato, more.

On *more*, the hand hit goes behind the back. The rhyme is repeated until all hands except one are eliminated. That person is "It."

In Ohio, a choosing rhyme goes:

As I went up the apple tree,
All the apples fell on me.
Bake a pudding, bake a pie,
Did you ever tell a lie?
Yes, you did. You know you did.
You broke your mother's teapot lid.
L-I-D spells lid, *and out you* go!

Some shorter rhymes are:

Doggie woggie, please step out
One, two, three, four, five, out!

Twenty horses in a stable.
Ten got out.
One, two, three, four, five,
Six, seven, eight, nine, ten, get out!

A B C D E F G H
I J K L M N O P
Q R S T U and you *are* out!

Monkey, monkey, bottle of beer,
How many monkeys have we here?
One, two, three, four, five, and out!

Inka, binka, bottle of ink,
The cork fell out, and you stink.
You. Y-O-U, you!

In baseball-type games, Toss the Bat is the method of choosing which team bats first and more importantly, who gets to choose his team players first. It involves a bat or, in Stickball, your mother's stolen mop handle or broomstick.

The captain tosses the bat to the opposing captain, who catches it firmly in either hand. Then, the tosser grabs the bat tightly above the other's hand. The first captain places his hand, then the second captain, and so forth until the top of the bat is reached. The player holding the top has to swing the bat around his head three times and then hold it at arm's length so that the other chooser can kick at it as violently as possible. If he holds on to it, he goes first and chooses first. If the other player succeeds in kicking it from his hand, then he goes first.

After one or more of these, you are in or out, up first or batting last, with the good guys or the bad guys, the Hunter or the Hunted, "It" or not.

And then the games begin.

SIDEWALKS

Miss Lucy had a baby.
She named him Tiny Tim.
She put him in the bathtub
To see if he could swim.
He drank up all the water.
He ate up all the soap.
He tried to eat the bathtub,
But it wouldn't go down his throat.

Miss Lucy called the doctor.
Miss Lucy called the nurse.
Miss Lucy called the lady with the alligator purse.
Mumps said the doctor.
Measles said the nurse.
Nothing said the lady with the alligator purse.
Miss Lucy punched the doctor.
Miss Lucy kicked the nurse.
Miss Lucy paid the lady with the alligator purse.

THE BEST OF our current crop of sidewalks, I'm told, consists of three parts gravel, two parts sand, and one part cement mixed with just the right amount of water to create the muddy mass that ultimately is smoothed and troweled into a sidewalk. Like tulle and lace, sidewalks come by the yard, not the thirty-six-inches-to-a-yard yard, but the mixed, poured, and finished concrete yard, which is ten feet long, four feet wide, and four inches deep. Which measures two and one-half sidewalk squares, which of course is four by four feet.

Wrong. Or rather, just half right.

Four-by-four sidewalk squares are suburban sidewalks. City sidewalk squares are five by five feet. Or at least they were once. Why have we foreshortened our sidewalks? Hard to say, except that if sidewalks are placed within the same framework as our new houses, a correlation can be supposed. Once houses had dining rooms; now they have L-shapes. Once there were spacious living rooms; now there are cramped family rooms from which the youngest members of the family are usually barred. We had parlors; now we have enclosed patios and Florida rooms. It's all of a piece.

I mean, if we can make a living room into a family room that's not lived in, we certainly can make sidewalks one foot shorter all round. Who would know? Who would care?

Generations of Pottsie players, that's who, and Handball and Box Ball addicts, whose whole games and strategies have been geared to the five-foot sidewalk square. It's like moving Rod Laver's end line in several feet. My Lord!

Nor is that the only change.

Of utmost importance to sidewalks is the amount of water that is added to the gravel, sand, and cement. Too much water makes for weak sidewalks, which for a time look as terrific as strong sidewalks, but which flake and powder and crack almost immediately after the concrete man has received his final payment.

Strong sidewalks—oh, we *did* have strong sidewalks—stay intact for years, yielding neither to the onslaughts of rain, snow, shovel, and rake nor to the expansion of tree trunks. Weak sidewalks make very bad playing fields. Strong sidewalks, worn smooth with the years, provide as fine a playing surface for sidewalk games as the Houston Astrodome with its carpet-smooth plastic grass does. After all, the prime consideration of our youth, of anyone's youth, was where to play. If you lived in a city, then the existence of a level, crack-free stretch of sidewalk was a blessing.

We had, I recall, such regard for sidewalks that few of us succumbed to the very great urge to put our thumbprints and palm and sneaker prints—not to mention initials, hearts, and arrows—into still-wet concrete when it had been put down. That was *caring*.

Of course, cracks were useful (when walking to school) to leap over while shouting,

Step on a crack and break the Devil's back.
Step on a line, break the Devil's spine!

and shoving and tripping your friends to make *them* step on a crack. Except for that, however, intact sidewalks were desired to bounce balls on, to skip upon, to pitch and catch on, to play jacks and cards on.

If you were playing **Shot for Shot** standing around with your buddies

29

trading on-the-arm punches, then the sidewalk was a fight ring. If you were part of a **Chinese Twist** line, in which one after the other, players holding on to each other's hands contorted themselves into human pretzels without letting go, then the sidewalk was a wrestling mat.

The sidewalk in front a selected stoop was the gathering place each spring for the bottle cap–collecting rite. During the winter, we carefully collected all the bottle caps we could find, removed the cork linings (which were inexplicably saved) then brought them to the stoop. After an official counting, a winner was declared, and it was his right to lead all collectors to a rooftop or a fire escape and direct the spilling of the hundreds of caps to the sidewalk in one shattering deluge. Good fun, and almost as noisy as a garbage can smashing against a brownstone stoop in the night.

The sidewalk was home for the spaldeen and for the little hard-as-a-rock solid black rubber handball, as well as for the pottsie.

POTTSIE

By anybody's odds, the most widely known and remembered sidewalk game is Pottsie. Oh, people from such places as Boston and Nottingham call it **Hopscotch;** and in Chicago, it is **Sky Blue.** In parts of the Far West, it comes out **Potsie** (pronounced *Poh-tse*); but for most of the rest of us, it is **Pottsie,** or **Pottsy,** or **Potsy,** a game of demanding, exacting rules, played best by thin people with good balance who take the trouble to wear sneakers that are not too smoothly worn around the balls of the feet and provide the best stopping power.

The **Pottsie** court is drawn with chalk on the sidewalk like this:

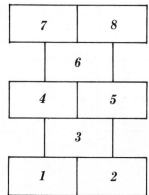

or like this:

or for those, like the English, with narrow sidewalks:

start	out	1	2	3	4	5	7 / 6	8	9	out	10

or, for that matter, for those with rather wide sidewalks:

4	9	19	6	13
11	17	3	20	12
8	2	5	7	16
1	10	15	18	14

or for those with a bent for design:

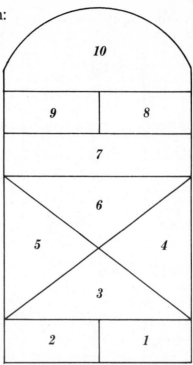

The version above was imported by Italian immigrants. Because of the shape of the 10 area, it is called **The Bell**. In Austria, it is called **The Temple**. In both countries, 8, 9, and 10 are called, respectively, "Inferno," "Purgatory," and "Paradise," which is rather a nice way to regard Pottsie —as kind of a passage to heaven.

or like these:

9	
7	8
6	
4	5
3	
1	2

9	10
7	8
6	
4	5
3	
1	2

or for the Gothically inclined:

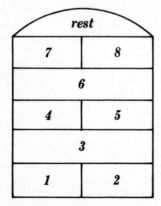

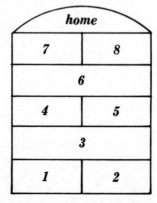

Pottsie.

In most other countries, the versions that have domes, bells, rests, or homes call these areas "the Pot." But variations in design abound; the last space may be a triangle or simply an elongated box. Often, the design is like a ladder's rungs:

10	9	8	7	6	5	4	3	2	1

or simply:

1	2	3	4
5	6	7	8

or finally, for those with exotic taste:

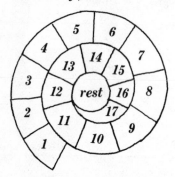

In all Pottsie games, the essential aim is to own as many numbered areas as possible, and whatever the shape of the chalked court, the games are played similarly everywhere. In Algiers and Moscow, Madrid and Mexico City, Pottsie varies only in name. In Point Hope, Alaska, for example, recent visitors saw Pottsie courts etched in ice and Eskimo children hopping from square to square precisely as you and I did.

The pottsie itself is important to the game. It is generally agreed that oblong pieces of slate chipped out of someone's patio or decorative walk make the best pottsies. But flat stones are used, as are nests of paper clips linked together, the glass bases and lips of soda bottles sanded smooth by rubbing them tediously over macadam or manhole covers, the tops of peanut butter jars, bottle caps, and skate keys. Skate keys are almost as highly regarded as slate chips.

A player places his or her toes right at the 1–2 line (or, in the English version, at Start) and tosses his pottsie into the 1 square. The player then hops on one foot into 2 and 3, landing with his left foot in 4 and his right foot in 5, then right-foot it into 6, and with both feet into 7 and 8. He then jumps, twisting his body and landing with his feet in 7 and 8 again but with his body facing Start. He then hops back to the start in the same way and bends over, with one foot in 2, to pick his pottsie up out of 1. The pottsie is then thrown into the 2 square, and the hopping through the diagram begins again. If a pottsie is in a square, it is out of bounds to all players. Where there are 9 and 10, the game is just extended. Home and Rest are areas in which to laze about, loll, and rest your arches until screamed at by other players to get on with it.

Once a player traverses the Pottsie court, he goes back down the court from 10 to 1, turns his back, and tosses his pottsie over his shoulder. Where it lands becomes his property and is marked off with his initials.

4	5 ME

Urban playing fields.

Thereafter, no other player can place a foot in that square, but the owner can loll about in it on two feet if he wishes. The player owning the most squares at the conclusion of the game is the winner. He is also the winner if he forces his opponents to give up before that: for example, by owning 3 through 6 and forcing the other players to one-foot hop from 2 to 7. Players go in rotation (the order chosen with "One potato, two potato") and continue until they fail to land their pottsie in the appointed square, fail to drop their over-the-shoulder pottsie into an unowned square, fail to jump from square to square properly, or lose their balance, which is quite frequent. One without balance is always a Klutz and is a much-sought-after opponent. The English version, with that nastily placed Out box between 9 and 10 is, according to Nottingham correspondent C. E. Meakin, very irritating.

Hopping from square to square in the twenty-square Pottsie game and in the snail-shaped version is most difficult—especially if the rules of the day are one-foot hopping—particularly when boxes begin to come under ownership. The game is to be remembered fondly as a source for considerable crying and swearing.

The ultimate refinement of Pottsie is the Chinese version called **Gat Fei Gei,** which translates literally into "One Foot Jumping Flying Machine," or more simply, **Airplane.** It is still seen on the streets of the Chinatowns of both New York and San Francisco. The court looks like this:

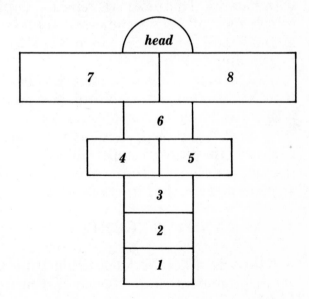

As in other Pottsie games, the players progress through the numbered squares. Then, after a player completes his series of eight, he stands with his toes at the edge of 1 and throws his piece of roof tile, which in China was the common pottsie, at the Pig's Head. Why it is called Pig's Head nobody seems to know; it just is. The player then hops through the boxes as in the regular game. He then has the choice of reaching over his back (without looking) to retrieve his tile or reaching through his legs upside down to do the same. If his hand touches the ground outside of the limits of the Pig's Head, he loses his turn. If he succeeds in touching and picking up his tile, he is rewarded with square 1. This process is repeated until all the numbered squares are owned. As in all Pottsie games, other players cannot hop into owned boxes, but magnanimous owners can mark off "sidewalks" inside the boxes to permit the dipping of a toe.

A player may, of course, step into a box he owns, but only with both feet. If he should forget and hop into his own property on one foot only, his "house" is declared "burned down" and the square is once again on the open market.

Once all squares are accounted for, the Pig's Head is divided into four parts, and the players compete for those four parts in the same way they went after the body of the airplane, so it is obviously possible to lose the airplane and win the Pig's Head. Clear?

THINGS AND CATEGORIES

In parts of New York, particularly in Brooklyn and Queens, Pottsie is often a preliminary to another chalk-marked game usually called **Things** or **Categories.**

The playing court is rather simple and standard, although drawn on the sidewalk with chalk like Pottsie, and the game is a test of mind rather than balance. In New York City, the winner at Pottsie earns the right to go first at Things. The courts look like this:

fruits	cars
colors	trees
actors	birds
games	cigarettes

or this

cars	teachers
colors	actors
boys	cigarettes
girls	states
soaps	flowers

start

Instead of a pottsie, the player uses his or her spaldeen. He rolls it gently into the lower left box (Games in the first example and Soaps in the second), then hurries to catch it while it is still in the box. Then, the player walks through the eight (or ten) boxes, bouncing the ball once in each and announcing the name of a game (or a soap) at the same time. The rules dictate that ball, foot, and word be simultaneous. It is not unusual for players to sit on the curbs thumbing through discarded magazines—*Saturday Evening Post* in my day, perhaps *Rolling Stone* today—for inspiration while they wait their turns. No hesitation is permitted, and if a beat is missed, the player loses his turn. If he or she makes it through the playing court, then it is on to the next box, clockwise.

The eventual winner is the player who goes through all eight (or ten) categories first. If the player's name is, say, Elena, she is entitled to spell her name out in the corners of the boxes (E in games, L in Actors, E in Colors, N in Fruits, A in Cars). Obviously, whoever goes through the field first will have his or her name spelled the most times.

Another, more difficult variation is to go through the alphabet while traversing the boxes, naming an item in each category beginning with the chosen letter. Thus, the walker bounces his way through a litany such as, "B, Bingo; B, Burt Lancaster; B, blue; B, berries; B, Buick; B, birch, B, blue jay; B, Benson and Hedges." Winning is more difficult because another discipline, the alphabet, is imposed on the mind. But the players don't think of it that way at all. Basically, if you make it through the boxes, you are smart. If you don't, you are dumb.

RUSSIA

The spaldeen is basic to many, many sidewalk games. It is the sidewalk metronome by which scores of rhyming games are consciously metered; it is a substitute football, basketball, baseball, and soccer ball; it is a discus, a missile. It is, quite simply, a necessity. A tennis ball, no matter how new, no matter that you can boast of having stolen it at considerable risk that very morning by reaching through the chicken wire of a neighborhood court, is no substitute for the spaldeen. It is right for sidewalks, bounces beautifully on concrete, and is terrific for bouncing that goes with

One, two, three, a-nation,
I received my confirmation
On the day of declaration
One, two, three, a-nation

and with

A my name is Alice,
I come from Alabama,
And in my basket I carry Apples.
B my name is Betty,
I come from Boston,
And in my basket I carry Bananas

and with

> *Pepper, salt, mustard, cider*
> *How many bullets killed the Kaiser?*
> *Ten, twenty, thirty, forty,*
> *Fifty, sixty, seventy*

and with

> *Mother, Mother, I am sick.*
> *Send for the doctor, quick, quick, quick.*
> *Doctor, Doctor, shall I die?*
> *Yes, my dearie, by and by.*
> *How many carriages shall I have?*
> *Ten, twenty, thirty, forty*

The spaldeen is also essential to such complicated sidewalk-wall games as Russia. Draw a line in chalk about four feet from the base of a wall, usually brick, brownstone preferred, and play this way:

For "onesies," throw the ball against the wall and, standing behind the line, catch it before it hits the ground. Do this once.

For "twosies," throw it against the wall, let it bounce once in the area between the wall and the line, then catch it. Do this twice.

For "threesies," toss the ball at the wall and clap, catching it before it hits the ground. At the first throw, clap once; at the second, clap twice; at the third, clap three times. Clap before catching the ball and without allowing it to bounce.

For "foursies," throw the ball and wind your hands four times bobbin-

Russia..."onesies."

Russia...'Threesies.'

fashion before catching it.

For "fivesies," throw the ball around and under one of your legs against the wall, then catch it before it bounces. Do this five times.

"For "sixsies," place one hand against the wall, then throw the ball from under and around the arm, bounce it against the wall, clap your hands twice, and then catch it. Do this only once because once is enough.

For "sevensies," throw the ball against the wall, clap your hands once in front of you, then once behind your back, then catch the ball before it hits the ground. Do this seven times.

For "eightsies," throw the ball against the wall, clap your hands, cross your chest, clap again, then catch the ball. Do this eight times.

For "ninesies," throw the ball, clap, bring up your bent knee so you can touch your ankle, clap again, then catch the ball. Do this nine times.

For "tensies," bounce the ball nine times on the ground; then, as it comes up on the ninth bounce, slap it against the wall and catch it before it hits the ground. Do this only once. It is relatively easy, presumably on the theory that if you get that far, you deserve a break. The first player to successfully go through all ten challenges is the winner.

Why the game is called Russia, I don't know. In the Bronx, it is known as **Wall Ball**; and in Queens, as **Seven Up**. In Seven Up, there are only seven steps. Variations include one for "threesies" (slap the ball, Handball fashion, three times against the wall before catching it,) and one for "sevensies" (throw the ball, spin your body around, and return to face the wall in time to catch the ball). Whatever its name, it is a test of considerable endurance. And it is not so much the joy of winning that spurs one on, but rather the terror of losing. This is because losers are subjected to **Cans Up**.

CANS UP

In this game, which is less a game than one of delicious tortures concocted by children on the streets, the player who comes in last in any of the varieties of Russia, is obliged to press himself, face inward, against a wall while the other players aim their spaldeens, one at a time at his rear end. Adding to the winners' joy are the remarks that precede the throws, designed for suspense and which can well be imagined—but not printed.

As with most games, there are regional variations of Cans Up, which is native to the Bronx. These include **Ass Ball** (Philadelphia), **Moony-Ups** (Queens), in which the loser has to bend at the waist and present his posterior to its best advantage for the winners, and **Bootys-Up** (concocted on the Lower East Side of Manhattan), in which the loser faces the wall, raises his arms as if he is about to be frisked, and stands waiting for the three to five shots alloted to each winner. Fun.

Up and ready . . . or not.

DODGE BALL

Another piece of mischievous sadism is called Dodge Ball. It is also simple and direct, but it differs from **Cans Up** and its variations in that it gives its victims both a fighting chance and opportunities to turn the tables. Any number can play, but the ideal is, as I recall, six. One player is chosen to be thrower; the other five, throwees. The Dodge Ball court is simply five sidewalk squares; where they meet a wall, the joints between squares are extended, via chalk, up the wall. The thrower stands in the street away from the sidewalk, about twenty feet away, and is free to throw his spaldeen at anyone he choses. Those being thrown at can jump, twist, duck, or move anyway they like to avoid being hit—but not out of their assigned areas.

If a player is hit, 1 point is marked against him; 3 points and he is out of the game. Not at all bad. But there is an advantage to staying in. If you succeed in catching the thrown ball, then you become the thrower and the tosser takes your place as well as any points you have accumulated up to that time. Good hands as well as a tough hide are essential.

Hit and you're "It."

TIRE GAME

Out in the Brownsville section of Brooklyn, a boys-only game, invented a quarter of a century ago, and again characterized by the get-your-buddy theme, flourishes. It is called the Tire Game and like Dodge Ball, it is simple and direct. The basic equipment needed is a discarded automobile tire, which with city children is the standard replacement for a rolling hoop.

One player is chosen to be "It," and he rolls the tire down the sidewalk. Every other player has to bow his legs and leap upward, straddling the tire as it rolls through his legs. He is not permitted to touch it. If the other players are successful, the player who is "It" stays "It." He is likewise "It" if the roll is a poor one that waddles into the gutter before all the players get their chance to leap over it. On the other hand, if a player fails to clear the tire, he becomes "It" and he is so dubbed by the previous "It." How? Well, the former "It" grabs the tire and, discus-fashion, whirls about with it and lets it fly at the new "It," who stands about ten feet away. Tire is an excellent source of unexplainable black-and-blue marks.

I DECLARE WAR ON

Less injurious but essentially the same is the game of I Declare War On in all its infinite variations.

As played in New York City in the 1940s, it was an exercise in rather basic patriotism played by anywhere from five to ten youngsters. The player chosen to be "It" was given a spaldeen and was America. It was his privilege to name all the other players as countries. Obviously, if there was someone you didn't like, he or she became Germany, Italy, Japan, (for the more sophisticated, Vichy France), or anybody else construed as being part of the Axis. With more players came names of Allied countries and neutrals, but this was never a problem because you simply didn't declare war on your friends—not in the 1940s anyway.

America asked if every country was ready and, after being told yes, threw the spaldeen straight up in the air as high as possible and shouted, "I declare war on—Japan," as all the other players scattered. They continued running until America caught the ball; then, they froze wherever they were and in whatever position they happened to be in. America then let fly his spaldeen at Japan. If Japan was hit, he became "It" and America joined the pack. It is easy to see that in this game it was to one's advantage to be, say,

Afghanistan, because who was angry at Afghanistan in 1945?

A Brooklyn variation dictated that America stand on a manhole cover and bounce the ball while teasingly intoning, "I declare war on, I declare war on, I declare war on—*Germany*," at which point the others scattered. The game was the same from then on, with numerous spaldeen-raised hickeys blooming on arms, legs and buttocks.

Yet another version involves construction of a chalk diagram with the names of planets ringed around a central area for "It":

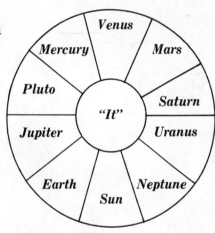

Here, "It" has to bounce the ball as hard as he can; and as it hits the ground, "It" declares war on whichever planet he choses. The bounce is also the signal for the other planets to scatter about their concrete universe and then to freeze and await their spaldeen meteor.

In the Jamaica Plains section of Boston, the game varies and is called either **Diamonds and Rubies** or **Movie Stars**. A chalk circle is drawn on the sidewalk, and "It" stands inside, throws the spaldeen in the air, and calls

The end of detente.

out "diamond" or any other gem (or "Clark Gable" or whoever). The difference between Boston and Brooklyn is that the person who has been called has to catch the ball while the other players, including "It", scatter. As soon as the ball is caught, the catcher screams "Freeze!" Then he has the privilege of throwing the ball at anyone he choses after taking three giant steps toward the chosen one. If the new person is hit, he becomes "It." Otherwise the thrower goes into the chalked circle.

Yet another version, played in Philadelphia, is **Baby in the Air**. The players are neither movie stars, precious stones, planets, nor countries; they are merely numbers. "It" throws the ball up and calls a number. When the player whose number has been called catches the ball he is allowed to throw it at anyone he choses after taking three jumping steps. If he hits his victim, the victim is awarded a *B*. This goes on until one person has *baby* spelled out on his hide; he is then eliminated from the game.

In Manhattan, Baby in the Air becomes **Spuds**. It is essentially the same game, but the person hit with the ball receives an *S* and then the other letters spelling out *spuds*.

However, if the thrower misses his intended victim (who, although he cannot move his feet after "Freeze" is shouted, can bob, weave, duck, or whatever to avoid being hit), the thrower gets a letter. The first one to have *spuds* spelled out against him either goes **Under the Mill** (which means crawling on one's hands and knees through the legs of the other players as they whack you on the behind), or stands face against a tree while the others throw the spaldeen at you.

COIN AND STICK

Two less violent sidewalk games that require more aim than brawn are Coin and Stick, also known as **Hit the Coin** and **Hit the Stick.** Again, all that is needed is your spaldeen and a relatively level, uncracked, two-square stretch of sidewalk and a coin (usually a penny, but a nickel or dime will do) or a Good Humor ice cream stick.

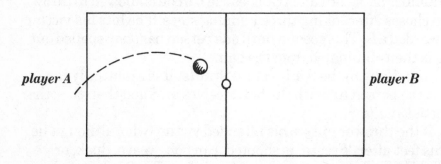

player A

player B

Each player stands at either end of the sidewalk boundary. The coin or stick is placed directly in the center at the seam of the two concrete squares. The object is to hit the coin or stick with the spaldeen, to make it flip over, and to move it toward your opponent. Each hit means 1 point, a flip is 2 points. Twenty-one points wins the game. In Coin, whoever is closest to the coin when his mother calls him in for supper gets to keep it.

A penny . . .

...or a quarter, the game's the thing.

Out in Flushing (in the New York City borough of Queens) where I grew up, Stick is played with an ice cream pop as the stake. Losing is bad because it means foregoing your evening treat for a day and watching your opponent eat not only his pop but the second one he bought with the nickel you got from your mother or father. Bad.

BOX BALL

Coin and Stick are simpler variations on the theme of sidewalk tennis. All such games utilizing the customary five-foot squares of the sidewalk as a court from which to serve, volley, and defend are really the city child's inventive and inexpensive way to play tennis or ping-pong. Box Ball and its refinements are more intricate. The court is two sidewalk squares; the base lines are the limits of the concrete; the joint between the two squares is the imaginary net.

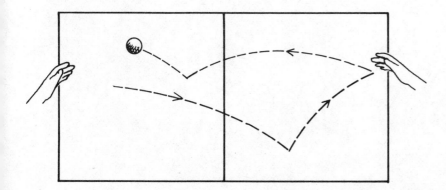

The players do "odds-or evens" for the right to serve. The ball is hit with the open palm into one's opponent's box; after a bounce, it is returned with a

slap. Players must stay out of the playing court. The first player to get 21 points wins, and as in tennis, it is necessary to win by 2 points. Thus a game of, say, 52 to 50, although not usual, is possible. Nor is this game a simple slapping back and forth.

A point is gained when your opponent either fails to return a shot into your box or misses a shot entirely. The winner of the point always serves. In Queens, we always played for stakes that ranged from a nickel or a dime to an ice cream to a number of prized marbles, perhaps to an aggie, (the prized agate marble used as a shooter).

Techniques of serving and returning were developed, for example, slapping at the ball with a downward, chopping motion that skims against one side of the spaldeen even as it is being returned. Unbelievable "English" (the art of producing illogical bounces by hitting the ball with sideswipes of the palms) is possible, and the demands made on players by soft, crazy-bouncing shots and wicked, low, just-inside-the-line returns are often unnerving.

BOX BASEBALL

A sophisticated variation of Box Ball is Box Baseball, which stretches across three sidewalk squares:

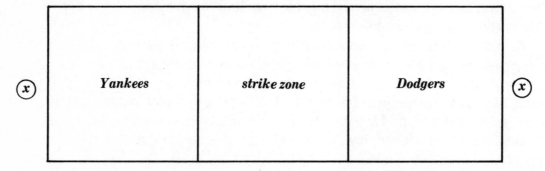

With this arrangement, an entire nine-inning game between the Dixie Walker Dodgers and the Joe DiMaggio Yankees was possible or, today, the Bobby Bonds Yankees and the Steve Garvey Dodgers). No slapping the spaldeen back and forth in this game. Only pitching skill is involved and the ability to squeeze your spaldeen so that you throw nothing but knuckle balls, which, with the spaldeen, is "English" personified.

As William Weiss, who apparently was one of the aces of Box Baseball over in Brownsville (Brooklyn) in the forties, wrote, it was "a game of skill and strategy favoring double-jointed players with long legs and arms, and

The World Series—sidewalk style.

pianist's fingers."

The team up first —let's say, the Yankees—in the person of perhaps the best player in the neighborhood (in the 1940s and 1950s if you were the best, you were automatically the Yankees) grasps his spaldeen like a knuckle ball and kind of squirts it at his opponent, the Dodgers. To be a fair ball, it has to pass over the strike zone and land in the opponent's box. The opponent, who has to stand outside the box, is required to catch the ball on one bounce. If he does, it is counted as an out. Catching a ball on the fly is also an out. If he fails to, every bounce adds to the quantity of the base hit. Thus, two bounces means a single; three, a double; four, a triple; and more than that, a home run. If the ball bounces in the strike zone or on one of the seams separating the zone from the two opposing boxes, it is a strike. Two strikes are out. Two outs constitute an inning.

The best players are able to squirt the ball just above ground level, just past the boundary between the strike zone and the opponent's square, with so much "English" on it that it bounces in the square and then snaps back in reverse fashion, virtually assuring a home run. Very often in Box Baseball, players refuse to play unless a referee is present because the arguments over balls that are close to or on the separating lines (called "liners" or "linsies") are fierce and often physical—which is to be expected in a World Series.

In the Bronx, in front of a house that everybody knows of as Gildember Avenue because the name Gildember is etched in granite above the entrance, Box Baseball is known as **Curves**. It requires even more skill and is governed by an even more intricate set of rules.

The playing field is the same, but in this game, when the Yankees pitch to the Dodgers, a catch is not required. Instead, the opponent has to slap at the ball, as in Box Ball. If the pitcher catches it on a fly, it is an out; if he misses it, then one bounce is a single; two, a double; and so on.

In this version, the center no-man's-land box is a ball box rather than a strike zone. If the pitcher throws the ball in there, it is a ball. If he throws it into his opponent's box and the opponent fails to swing at it, it is a strike. If the batter hits the ball into the center box, it is considered an out. Thus, bases on balls, unknown in the Brooklyn game, are possible in the Bronx game. Batting skill is required. And there are many ways to make an out. Also, in the Gildember Avenue game of Curves, a regulation baseball structure is preserved: three outs to an inning, nine innings to a game. Altogether, it would seem, a more demanding game than the Brooklyn Box Baseball. The one constant, however, is the ability to put "English" on the spaldeen, which means that a good pitcher can beat a good hitter every time.

Come to think of it, isn't that what Casey Stengel said repeatedly?

FOUR-WAY BOX BALL

Another extension of basic Box Ball is Four-Way Box Ball, also known as **Four Ball**, which is played by four players. It is limited by the nature of the court to parts of cities that have wider avenues and wider sidewalks. Four Ball flourishes in the better brownstone sections of the city, where there is seldom a band of dirt between the sidewalk and the curb; instead, there is a double or a triple sidewalk. The Four Ball court consists of two sidewalk squares by two sidewalk squares and looks like this.

The four players usually straddle the corners of the four squares, with player 1 usually the server. He hits the ball with his hand into the box to his right (4 in this case) on the serve. Then, the player in square 4 is free to hit it, after it bounces, into any box he chooses. The ball is kept in play until a miss or a faulty serve earns the goofer a point, and 6 points means you are eliminated. After a point, all the players move over one box, clockwise, and the player now in square 1 becomes the server. Once a player is eliminated, his box becomes out-of-bounds territory, or Dead-Man's Land, and the ball cannot be hit into it. This is a tough game and full of surprises because you are never sure where a player will slap the spaldeen. As in all Box Ball games, "English" is important. Falling on your face while trying to slap at a reverse-bouncing ball almost always earns not only a point but derision.

In this game, there are two variations: **Funsies** and **Killers.** Because of the four players and the constant element of surprise, it is agreed upon beforehand that a game will be either Funsies (no vicious smashes allowed) or Killers, which was always short and swift. Often, a fine server simply keeps his serve, blasting his way through his three opponents eighteen times. Killers games are money games, and to serve is an almost overriding advantage.

HANDBALL

Perhaps no game is as truly urban or has had so great a mystique grow up around it as Handball. Not the athletic-club kind, with courts surrounded by four walls, where paunchy businessmen exercise at lunch, but the one-wall kind. To be precise, the eastern-seaboard style. Or to be more precise, the Handball that has come to be regarded as New York Jewish Handball and has spawned the likes of the Obert brothers, Steve Sandler, Vic Hershowitz, Joel Skolnick (who is not a handballer of the caliber of the others because of intrinsically bad knees but who is sort of the unofficial historian of the cult), and others to whom Sunday mornings in Coney Island at the foot of Ocean Parkway and anywhere along Avenue P is the Super Bowl, the World Series, and the Olympics, gift wrapped. "In the YMCAs they play four-wall. In the yeshivas and against the synagogue walls its always one-wall."

For Jewish children who came to this country and settled with their families in New York's Lower East Side or across the river in Brooklyn's Williamsburg, as well as for the children who were born in these ghettos, Handball is more than a game; it is tradition. It is essentially a poor peoples' game (as are most street and city games), requiring nothing save a wall, a concrete playing surface, a black solid rubber ball, and for the more affluent, a pair of tight leather gloves. In the first part of this century and on through the depression years, even into the 1950s, Handball was virtually the im-

Handball is not for novices.

migrant's only game. There was no money for the stadium; money was for books and food, quite often in that order. It was a game that could be played against the wall of one's own tenement, on one's own sidewalk, and it has lasted to this day. But like other aspects of our lives, as the Jewish community became assimilated, fluid, and dispersed, Handball, as one aspect of that community's life, became less popular, less important, less mystical. Yet, it still hooks thousands of players who doggedly cling to one-wall Jewish Handball, which one great player, Steve Sandler has said, "will be like the Buffalo" in another twenty years.

For one-wall Handball, the sidewalk playing surface should be reasonably level; the one-wall courts in city parks are usually pretty good. The best walls are smooth, of either unrippled concrete or unetched limestone. But a brick wall, worn with age and layered over with cement paints and waterproofing that gives it a certain smoothness, is okay, too.

The ball, however, must be precise. It is of black rubber, solid, $1\frac{7}{8}$ inches in diameter (a thirty-second of an inch variation is tolerated). It weighs 2.3 ounces and has a rebound capacity of 62 to 65 inches when dropped from a height of 100 inches at a temperature of 68 degrees. Yes sir. Any dedicated Handball player is prepared to weigh, measure, or drop in the name of purity.

Children play Handball with their spaldeens, but by their early teens, boys switch (graduated is the way they regard their transition) to the palm-splitting, callous-raising black solid rubber balls, which are never called anything but handballs. They used to cost about twenty-five cents; now they come (for the information of aficionados) packed two to a vacuum-packed can, are known as Seamless 555s and are two for ninety cents. Spaldeens and their not so highly regarded imitations (the pennsy and the pinky) are generally regarded as equipment suitable only for kids and ladies. To some, I expect, the ascendance to the black, solid ball was virtually a puberty rite.

Handball, New York Jewish style, is still one of the most popular urban games today. In New York, there are more than 2,000 handball courts stuck into parks to meet the demand. These are standard in size, actually a set of three twenty-by-twenty-foot concrete slabs, two set end to end and the third upended.

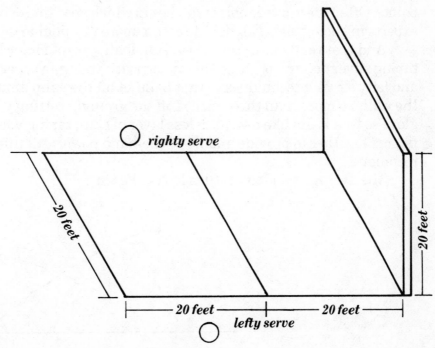

The rules are very simple. A player stands outside of the line court area and behind the line separating the courts to serve. He bounces the ball, then slaps it, on a fly, against the wall. The other player either waits for it to bounce once and then returns it to the wall with his own shot or hits it, on a fly, to the wall. If a ball hit by either player on a serve or on a return lands outside of the court area, the one who hit it badly is penalized and his opponent receives 1 point and the right to serve. Although 21 points wins the game, there are 11-point games. In any case, the winner has to win by 2 points. Often there are doubles matches in which good line drive hitters join experts in slicing and "English" to create more formidable teams.

And that really is all there is to Handball, except for such niceties as taping silver dollars to your palm underneath your glove; perfecting righty and lefty serving techniques so that balls jet off the palm almost straight to the wall, no more than three inches off the ground; wetting your leather glove so that it fits like a wrinkleless layer of skin; taping your two middle fingers together to provide middle-of-the-hand power. All this is considered technique.

The average handball return looks like this:

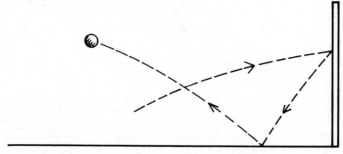

A fantastic shot is "killer":

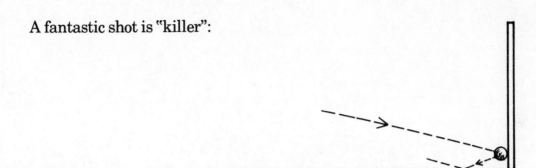

which hits exceedingly low on the wall, then bounces off almost in skimming fashion, making it virtually impossible to return.

And there is "Dying Swan":

which arches into the wall, just grazing it, then rebounds weakly, and dies, dribbling onto the court. Another shot that is almost impossible to return.

A failed attempt to make a great shot, a gamble (called a "choke" or a "crotch shot"), that lands exactly where the court meets the wall looks like this:

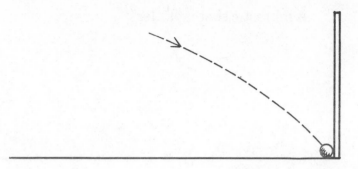

The fellow who has gambled loses 1 point. Often, however, it is worth the try.

Handball has *always* been played for some sort of stake (money; soda, later on, beer), and most players agree with Skolnick that they "can't ever remember *not* playing for *something*. Gambling was part of the whole thing. Even today the great players play for money. A buck a point, ten bucks a game, that's almost a for-funs game. It's not unusual to have $500 riding on a Handball match." Often, a young man in his late teens would play Handball for income. In a real sense, it was his job.

It is a game of anticipation, of wits, of continuously thinking while playing, and it requires split-second swiftness. A player has to be aware of his position, the position of his opponent, which way his opponent is moving, which way he is pretending to move, which hand his opponent is going to use to hit the ball.

Generally, the finest players can hit equally well with either hand; some also have the ability to serve splendidly with either hand. There are forehands, of course, even backhands slapped with the palm, but there is little of the grace one associates with tennis. Handball is rough, jerky, quick moving, fast stopping.

Often, nowadays, the Handball courts are used for sidewalk tennis or **Paddle Ball,** a burgeoning craze. Paddle Ball, played by the same rules as Handball but with a spaldeen and wooden paddles punched through with tiny holes, is a fast game, like Handball. But the paddles do not lend themselves to as much trick playing as the hands do, and the game is a diversion, not the object of dedication that one-wall Handball is. "I wouldn't want to build character with paddle ball," says Skolnick.

Paddle ball—Handball for sissies?

CHINESE HANDBALL

Those who are not gamblers, who do not have formal Handball courts or heavily callused hands play the everyday version of Handball (in which the stakes are ice cream pops) with a spaldeen on the sidewalk against any building wall. And although it may not be essential to molding characters, it is fast and fun.

All Handball rules apply, but the court is the standard city court: two sidewalk squares. A player serves to his opponent's square and has the spaldeen returned to his square off the wall. It is similar to Box Ball, except that a candy store or grocery wall is a needed ingredient.

A variation of Handball is Chinese Handball, which, like most sidewalk games, has simple and complex versions.

The first, which seems to be the kind favored in Queens and in the West Oak Lane section of Philadelphia, is virtually the same as sidewalk Handball. Usually, two players, each with a sidewalk square, play against each other for 21 points. The difference is that the spaldeen has to hit the ground *before* it hits the wall, like this:

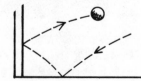

Requiring more agility and concentration is the version of Chinese Handball called **Kings**, played out in the Bay Ridge section of Brooklyn. Kings is Chinese Handball expanded to five players and of course extended to five sidewalk squares, like this:

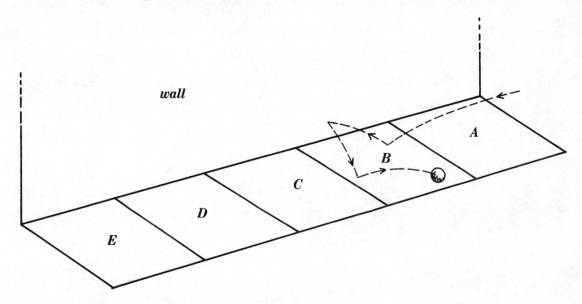

The player who serves (usually chosen by "odd finger") stands behind square A and hits the spaldeen into the B square, hitting the sidewalk first and then the wall. In the Bay Ridge version, the B player then has to hit it to C and so on, with E hitting it into D and on back up. Any player who misses or errs in any way receives 1 point and is moved back to square E. Acquiring

Chinese Handball—any wall will do.

11 points sends you out of the game. The player with the least number of points (in cases of fine head-to-head play) or the one who succeeds in eliminating the other players is the winner. Whoever is in the A square is considered Kings. He stays there and continues to serve until the player in B succeeds in forcing him to err while the ball is en route back up from the E end. A good server who can deliver low-trajectory "killers" usually does well and can on occasion literally run rings around those under him, eliminating them with his serve. The eventual winner then gets the opportunity of lining the other four players against the wall, "asses up," and throwing the spaldeen at their rumps.

The game is also called **Chinese Handball**, the server is Ace; the player in square B, King; the next, Queen; and so on down through the deck of cards. In this game, the server can send the spaldeen into any square he chooses; the same goes for the other players. Unlike Kings, there is no rotation involved. Ultimately, this is a game of fakery, with deceptive head and hip motions, ball slicing, smashing, and lobbing. This is the version that in parts of Pennsylvania is called simply **Ass Ball,** in honor of the ultimate punishment inflicted upon losers.

GERMAN

And then there is German, which seems to have originated in Paterson, New Jersey, where it is still played. It has its beginnings in Box Ball; a wall and a sidewalk are necessary, although the side of a set of brownstone steps will do nicely. A kind of horizontal court is set up and named for baseball hits, like this:

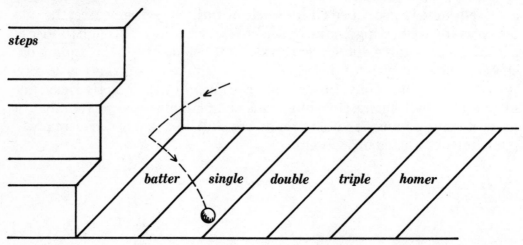

steps

batter   *single*   *double*   *triple*   *homer*

German is played with teams, usually three men to a side, but often two. A member of the batting team stands in the sidewalk square designated as the batter's box and slams or very lightly tosses his spaldeen against the wall (or step facade). The members of the other team stand in the squares marked Single, Double, and Triple and have to field the ball cleanly as it comes to them. If the player in the Single box muffs it, the batter receives a single. If he misses it entirely and then the second player, standing in the Double box, errs, it is a double. If the spaldeen gets by all three players, it is a home run. To catch a ball on the fly is an out.

The key member of each team obviously is the fellow who occupies the Single box. He has to be the best fielder, a Marty Marion of the sidewalk.

As in Baseball, there are innings, and a great to-do is made over who will be the Yankees, the Dodgers, or whichever teams are the pennant and series winners that year.

ERRORS

Sidewalk spaldeen games often use baseball terminology, rules, and limits. Such a game is Errors, a two-player game developed in the shadow of Yankee Stadium several decades ago.

Again, all that is needed is a stretch of sidewalk, moderately level and relatively free from cracks and those humps caused by the growth of sidewalk maple trees. The players stand perhaps twenty to thirty feet away from each other and toss a spaldeen back and forth, either on the fly or bouncing it on the ground. A player has to field the ball cleanly (like a baseball infielder), then toss it back to the other player as if pegging out a runner at first base. Definitely a showboater's game, a showcase to demonstrate whether a player can go to his right as well as Joe Morgan, is as good a fielding pitcher as Catfish Hunter, can pivot like Rod Carew. The player tries to foil the opposing fielder by putting backspin on the spaldeen, by skidding grounders close to the concrete, by throwing curve balls and sliders (we used to call them "down-and-outers").

An error costs the offender 1 point, and as in most such games, 21 points is the cutoff. In this case, the first one to get 21 loses.

RUNNING BASES

And then there is Running Bases, which can be as simple or as complicated as the players wish. Basically, two players throw a spaldeen back and forth along the sidewalk from a distance of about forty to fifty feet, although the distance is often shorter. A third player has to get from one sidewalk square, or "base," to the other (the squares the throwers stand in are the bases) without being tagged. Obviously he can't run faster than a thrown ball, but he can dodge back and forth, getting himself intentionally caught in a rundown, in the hope that either thrower will drop the ball or miss a throw. A sophisticated version of this is played on dirt and only by those who know how to slide into bases without fracturing an ankle. But the sidewalk version, which is the most common, is a simple test of both speed and agility. Often, two runners will run, as the ball goes back and forth.

If a runner succeeds in achieving four bases, he scores a run. The player with the most runs is the winner. If a runner is tagged out, he becomes a thrower and his place is taken by the player who has tagged him.

BASEBALL CARDS: A MEMORY

In most sidewalk games, the mind and the mouth are obviously the most necessary elements in creating and playing, with legs and arms following close on. Equipment—if you discount for the moment the ubiquitous spaldeen and the varieties of Pottsie—is virtually nonexistent, an unimportant consideration. Which is as it should be. However, there are exceptions.

*Such as Baseball Cards. This was also called **Plain Cards** because it was played not only with baseball cards but with G-man cards, war cards, comic book cards, even regular playing cards (two glued together to provide stiffness and weight). The simplest way of playing was for the two players involved to agree on a stake; seven cards was usually a fair test of ability. The one who went first flipped his cards (holding them lightly between his thumb and his other fingers) with a fluid motion along the side of his body from back to front onto the sidewalk. A good flipper could put down seven heads (with the war cards I remember most vividly, the atrocities committed by Japanese throughout China in the 1930s and 1940s were luridly portrayed, comic book fashion, on the heads side, and capsule accounts of decapitations were printed on the tails sides) or seven tails. The second player then had to match the pattern laid down by the first player, exactly, and it was winner take all. No par-*

tial winning; it didn't matter if a player matched the first six. All or nothing. In a very short time, a good flipper could compile a graphic history of the Far East, the roster of all major league baseball teams, and a compendium of the finest hours of J. Edgar Hoover and have all kinds of doubles with which to trade. A fine game, at which I was very good. Modestly, I say I am still.

In April, arms and fingers atrophied by winter must again become limber as rubber. The spine, arched forward from months of leaf raking and hunching over snow-shovel handles, must become bow-taut. Toes must be liberated from galoshes and thrust into sneakers. For the season—as always— begins tomorrow, and conditioning is expected to be instant. There is no five-week spring training in the sun at Sarasota or Clearwater to bake one's elbow into looseness, to make the hinge in the wrist become a spring. After school tomorrow, you are expected to be in condition at once, to flip your bubble gum baseball cards, and a serious player must flip as well for the April opener as he or she does at October World Series time.

Although there will necessarily be a lot of attention paid to the official opening of the baseball season tomorrow, more than passing interest should be paid to the unofficial, but equally important, opening of the Baseball Cards season. The flipping of baseball cards is a great, honorable, and national pastime that began simultaneously with the publication of the earliest baseball cards. As nearly as can be ascertained, this was around 1909, when the Talk of the Diamond cards were issued. The game flourished through the 1915 Crackerjacks series, the 1930s Goudey and Bowman bubble gum sets, and reached glorious fruition with the bubble gum cards of Fleers and Topps in the 1940s and 1950s. Kids, both boys and girls, are still flipping today. Although the game, the rules, and the terminology vary, baseball cards are flip-

Flipping—match it or lose it.

ped not only in metropolitan New York (where it is high art) but in Boston, Chicago, and Los Angeles and in the suburbs of America as well. Despite the fact that this great American game is pervasive, it is largely unheralded, a situation that this guide will attempt to remedy. Herewith a brief description of some of the rules, the techniques and the languages of the game.

The Collection

The ideal storage container for baseball cards has always been a cigar box. A Garcia y Vega box is remembered with nostalgic fondness. Shoe boxes are acceptable (although inferior) substitutes. Baseball heroes are carefully sorted into trading stacks, flipping stacks, and collecting stacks. Sorted cards are, of course, held firmly by rubber bands. Generally, doubles or even unwanted singles such as Frankie Baumholtzes and Clyde Kluttzes are traded or flipped. Other precious cards, Ted Williamses or Joe DiMaggios, are not flipped. They are kept forever—or at least until Mother cleans out the closet.

The Grip

The card, new and stiff, is held with all five fingers. They must rest on the long edges of the 3½-by-2½-inch card. The thumb is at the top edge; the other fingers are on the bottom; the card is positioned just back of the fingertips. Some players pass sandpaper across the fingertip whorls to smooth off winter calluses before flipping. This is not regarded as cheating.

The Stance

The best flippers stand like Joselito, Hemingway's favorite torero, as he planted himself for La Faena: feet together, weight balanced on the balls of the feet and the toes, spine arched backward, arms veed to the rear, pulling at the shoulder muscles. The store of cards to be flipped is held in the left hand and taken, one card at a time, into the right hand (reverse this for southpaws) and then flipped into competition.

The Flip

Like the perfect golf swing or tennis smash, a practiced flipping motion is the key to success in Baseball Cards competition. A player assumes The Grip and The Stance. Then, the arm is straightened and held downward, slightly to the rear of the player's own rear. The hand holding the card is palm forward. The flipper is required to look back over his or her shoulder and down at the hand as it moves forward a trifle, pendulum fashion, then into a modest backswing, and then forward again. The card is released into the motion-manufactured breeze just as the hand passes the thigh. If released with precision, the card will flip slightly backward in its journey to the ground, so that it comes to rest about half a foot behind the flipper and will always *be heads or tails, as demanded by the flipper. This is the most common flipping motion and the technique for several games, including Flips, Unmatch, and Fives and Tens.*

Flips

*This game, sometimes known as **Singles,** is your basic card-flipping con-*

test. The player flips his cards, trying to make them land in order. An oppos-
ing player gives a command (say, "Head, tail, tail, head"), and the flipper has
to tumble his cards in precisely that order or lose either the four cards involved
or an agreed-upon stake (today a Reggie Jackson or a Johnny Bench, in my
day a Spud Chandler or Phil Rizzuto). Singles is the same as Flips (it is be-
lieved to have originated in Richmond Hill) except that the demand for heads
or tails is made one card at a time. The stake is the card being flipped. Except
in cases where the flipper is a recognized neighborhood champ, it was always
best to be the house man in Flips or Singles because there were usually only a
few precision flippers per block. The rest generally flipped out of their
depth—and lost.

Unmatch

A perverse game, long a favorite in Park Slope, this is a variant of Sin-
gles. The flipper is required to unmatch the specific order given. Authorities
judge this a difficult game because a player not only has to flip his cards but
also must think. *Tough, tough.*

Fives and Tens

This game, highly demanding and brought to us from Chelsea, is re-
stricted to players with large resources because the minimum number of
cards wagered and flipped per turn is five, and more often ten. To play Fives
and Tens, you have to have the soul of a gambler. One player flips, say, ten
cards, and if he is good, very good, he might lay down ten tails. The player
who follows will then have to do the same. High drama. Now, let us say the

first player runs off nine tails, then fumbles and finishes with a head. If the matcher begins and fluffs his first card (if he tosses a head, something he obviously doesn't want), he is under pressure to flip nine tails in a row or lose all ten cards. Wow!

Three other Baseball Cards games are also well worth mentioning because of their popularity: Off the Stoop, Up Against the Wall, and Pitching. However, purists might say the games require no skill and are analogous to church bazaar wheels of chance, where success depends on luck.

Off the Stoop

Rarely if ever played in the suburbs, for obvious reasons, this game is believed to have originated in Brooklyn Heights, where it still thrives. The players kneel on the top step of a stoop. With their thumbs and middle fingers, they shoot baseball cards outward to the sidewalk. The object of this game is, not to match cards, but to cover your opponent's card with your own. If you cover the card, you own it. However, an important house rule, called "tippies," can change the fate of a game. A "tippy" occurs when a corner of one card barely touches a corner of another card. A "tippy" is considered a miss unless the house invokes the rule. "Tippies" is usually called on breezy days, when there is even less control over the cards than usual. The one to call it usually owns the stoop.

Up Against the Wall

This has been called the least mental of all card-flipping games; yet, it continues to enjoy great popularity. The card is slapped against a wall with

Up Against the Wall. Is it more luck than skill?

the palm, then the hand is pulled away quickly, and the card plummets to the ground. Competitions differ. The game can be played so that the cards cover other cards or so that cards can be matched. All serious players should observe one rule, however: They must never eat candy or ice cream before a game of Up Against the Wall because an overlooked sticky spot on a palm can ruin all strategies (such as they are).

Pitching

This game, a product of Manhattan's Upper West Side, requires a unique grip and flipping motion too complex to be described in detail here. Basically, however, the baseball card is slid between the first two fingers of the hand and, guided by the thumb, tossed toward a wall. Follow-through is very important. Pitching is definitely a game of technique, in which a downward thrust can result in a nose dive and too upward a toss can cause the card to flutter and die. Usually, three or five cards are thrown in succession. The player owning the card nearest the wall gathers up all the cards thrown. "Leaners" (cards leaning against a wall) are usually desirable, as in the game of horseshoes. However, house rules can be called to outlaw them.

I would like to conclude this guide to Baseball Cards with a reminiscence from my own playing days. During one competition (I think it was Off the Stoop), I had a "tippy." My card, a Heinie Manush, was barely touching an Honus Wagner. Unfortunately, "tippies" was not in force that day, so I lost. Only recently has this ancient defeat returned to haunt me. I have learned, believe it or not, that the Honus Wagner card is now worth about $1,500 to collectors. It seems that, originally, the card appeared in a pack of Sweet Caporal cigarettes, but it was withdrawn when Honus decided that the image he projected to American youth was not enhanced by appearing stuck into a pack of smokes. Only ninety-six Honus Wagners got into circulation, and there are only about ten or twelve around now, thus the $1,500 value.

All of which goes to show you what happens when you don't call "tippies."

TICKETS

Out in Flatbush, Brooklyn, trading cards are used in Tickets. Packs of trading cards or playing cards held together with rubber bands are used almost like pucks—thirty-two cards have the right heft.

A court using three sidewalk squares, is set up, and the first player sails or skims his pack of cards toward the back line of the third square. His opponent does likewise. The player whose pack is closest to the line then puts his knee down at the spot where his pack has landed and uses the pack to touch first the line and then his opponent's pack. Obviously, if packs are close by, it is an easy game to win (the stake is always an agreed-upon number of trading cards). But it is also easy to see that a good deal of strategy is involved and that it is one of the few games where it is best to go last, not first.

For example, if the first player is inches from the sidewalk line, then it is simply good sense for the next player to drop his pack directly in front of him, almost three sidewalk squares away. In this case, after the first player touches the line, he will have to toss his pack at the other pack and hope to land on top of it, which is the other way of winning. A game of position.

Up in Boston, always a scientific and innovative place, players take trading cards and dribble a tiny layer of molten solder along one edge. When the metal has hardened, the weighted cards are used to pitch against walls, the closest to the wall being the winner. This game is called **Solder,** of course.

BUTTONS

Related to both of these games is Buttons, in which political campaign buttons, baseball player buttons, or any of the thousands of round tin buttons (the kind with a straight pin on the back) are tossed at a wall. The player whose button is closest to the wall wins, and a "leanie" (a miraculous shot that sees the button leaning against the wall) earns a button bonus from each player.

Also used in games and highly prized by young collectors were those round Dixie cup tops, the ones with the tabs sticking up. It was necessary to take special pains to lift the top off the ice cream carefully to avoid bending it. Once the top was off, the girl with longest fingernails was in charge of peeling off the tiny tissue that separated the remnants of ice cream from the glossy, waxed, black-and-white picture of a movie star that grinned out at you.

These were no good at all for flipping, but they were good for trading. Boys, for example, would give two Clark Gables and an Alice Faye for one Manchurian massacre or for a neat account of how the FBI chased Clyde Barrow (illustrated) and feel that they had done well.

On occasion, these round tops would be scaled against the wall, as in Solder and Buttons. But they were difficult to control, aerodynamically unsound, and would veer off sharply up or down and thus were not valued by sharpshooters. But collectors of movie stars pictures valued them almost as highly as they did the four-by-six-inch glamour stills of stars that Woolworth's used to sell by the hundreds of thousands—you know, the kind they put in those cheap picture frames—and it was a mild coup to have both a four-by-six *and* a round photograph of your favorite star.

A movie star's picture wasn't the only prize provided by an ice cream cup; there was a possibility that a five-pointed star would be stamped on the bottom of the Dixie cup, to be found after all the ice cream had been spooned out. This entitled you to a free Dixie cup and of course another star's picture. Heaven.

These precious tops provided the inspiration for an after-supper guessing game—**Movie Stars.** Like most guessing-in-progression games, Movie Stars is a test of how well one has read the latest fan magazines, listened to Rona Barret, and kept one's collection of movie star pictures up to date.

The player who goes first begins with the letter *A* and gives the initials of a movie star whose first or last name begins with *A*. For example, *A.C.* would be Art Carney, perhaps *C.B.* would be Candice Bergen, and so on. If another player guesses from the initials, he then begins with *A* and continues until his selection is guessed. The first player to progress through the alphabet is the winner. Quick, give me a *Z*.

CHINESE JUMP ROPE

Rubber bands, the more exotic the better, are the ingredients needed for a simple version of Chinese Jump Rope. The game, although complex, is in a sense secondary to the rope itself, which is made from hundreds of rubber bands, of all colors and varying thicknesses, braided together to create a long length. The ends are then braided together, and the resulting circle is placed on the sidewalk.

A player then stands in the center and inches his feet outward, stretching the braid so that it ends up in a shape that can best be described as an oval flattened on the sides, like this:

There are various jumping tasks that must be performed while hopping in and out and around the stretched rubber bands. The most common game involves this progression: First jump into the enclosure on one foot, then hop out, then repeat this on the other foot. Then, it is into the enclosure with both feet, then out. Then, the jumper stands with both feet in the center, leaps up, spreads his legs so that his feet land just outside either end. Then, he jumps again, landing lightly on the curved ends, then up again, landing outside of the circle. Except for the touch down onto the oblong's ends, the jumper's feet are never permitted to touch the rubber bands. The first to progress through the various jumps successfully wins.

JACKS

And there is Jacks, which is usually played with six of these and one of these brightly painted

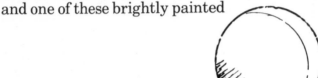

Some games are played with ten jacks. Actually, the manufacturers probably recognize the two forms of jacks because the five-and-ten packages usually consist of two balls and sixteen jacks. The jacks are usually lead and initially gold or silver colored, but these finishes gradually wear off with use. The ball is usually tiny (about the size of a Ping-Pong ball), usually of sponge rubber, and bright red or swirled with many colors.

The first player (definitely a girls-only game) places the six jacks (or ten) in the palm of her hand, then throws them sprawling. The jacks must be picked up in progression. The player throws the ball into the air (often maximum heights are established); then she picks up one jack, lets the ball bounce, and catches it with the same hand she used to pick up the jack. The steps are "onesies," "twosies," "threesies," and so on. In "onesies," the jacks are picked up one at a time. Then, it is two at a time, then three, and on up to six or ten. Once through this sequence, the player goes backward from "ten-sies" or "sixsies" to "onesies." The first to complete these steps is the winner.

This is the simple form of Jacks, or **Easies,** in which all kinds of concessions are made, generally to players who are not very good.

In "easies," a player can touch other jacks while picking up the one or ones she is after. Also allowed in this game is a maneuver permitting the player to toss the ball up, push two jacks away from each other, then pick them up singly after tossing the ball. This is called "movsies." Also allowed in "easies" is "popjack," which permits a player to shout, "Interference," if a ball hits a person or thing and to have another turn. "Easies" also permits the separation of "kissies" (two jacks touching after being thrown) and "haystacks" (one jack nestling inside another). Upon calling "kissies," or "haystacks," the player can pick up the touching jacks and drop them again before beginning her pickups.

In "strictsies," on the other hand, no "movsies" or "popjacks" or "interference" or "kissies" or "haystacks" are permitted. The player must progress through her pickups without touching any other jacks. There are no re-throws or do-overs.

However, a player can call, "Garbage," if she doesn't like the lay of her thrown jacks, and she is permitted to throw again. But this must be used judiciously because only three "garbage" calls are usually permitted.

In "strictsies," there is still another fillip that makes things difficult. If Jacks is being played near a curb and a jack or jacks falls into the street on the throw, any other player can call, "placies," and, with all the nastiness she can muster, can place it for example, right at the lip of the curb, where at

A game of "easies."

the slightest touch it will fall again and the player will lose her turn.

In many games of Jacks (either "easies" or "strictsies,") the player who goes through the one-to-six or one-to-ten progression and back first is the winner and is credited with 1 game. However, in many other games, these are only the preliminaries that precede "two-handed flip" and "one-handed flip." In the former, the player who has successfully picked up all her jacks holds them in the palms of her hands, then tosses them up, and as they begin coming down, flips her hands over and tries to catch as many of the jacks as possible on the backs of her hands. The number caught determines the game. For example, if she tosses up ten and catches three, with seven falling to the ground, then her game is automatically "threesies." One-Handed Flip is similar except that only one hand is used, which makes it more difficult.

A player continues to play as long as she picks up jacks and catches at least one. If she should fail to catch any jacks, the next player takes over. On the other hand, if she catches all the jacks, she is credited with another game. Obviously, the player with the most games when Mother calls everybody in to supper is the winner.

When winning goals are set (say, the first one to win five games is the winner), another game, called "Fancy," can be played. In it, the winner can dream up all sorts of Jacks exotica, such as bouncing the ball three times before picking up the jacks or lining them up so that they must be picked up one at a time in succession. The winner can make up any game she desires.

Expert players can do "Cherry in the Basket," which involves throwing the ball, picking up the jack, transferring it to the other hand, and permitting the ball only one bounce before catching it. Precision is paramount.

DROP THE HANDKERCHIEF

A necessary piece of equipment for Handkerchief or Drop the Handkerchief (known in my neighborhood as **A-Tisket A-Tasket**) is not, as you might imagine, a handkerchief. These are too precious, and if your mother thinks you're throwing them around on the sidewalk, there'll be hell to pay. Use an old sock filled with ashes and sealed with a rubber band.

A group of us would form a circle, facing inward. The player chosen to be "It" walks around the outside of the circle singing:

A-tisket, a-tasket,
A green and yellow basket.
I sent a letter to my love,
And on the way I dropped it.
I dropped it, I dropped it,
I dropped my yellow basket.
A little boy, he picked it up
And put it in his pocket.

At the conclusion of the song, the player holds up the sock and asks, "Do you see it, my children?" We'd all shout, "yes," then close our eyes. "It" would

105

make many noises as he or she walked around the circle, scraping, sniffing, snorting, humming, and then drop the sock and shout, "Look!" The other players looked behind them, and the one behind whom the sock lay had to pick it up, chase the dropper around the outside of the circle, and hit him or her with the sock, creating a nice ashy pattern on his clothing if possible, before the dropper took over the place in the circle vacated by the one with the sock.

If the fellow with the sock misses, he then becomes the chanter and the dropper. An amusing game, with that little touch of violence that characterizes most children's games and makes them all the more spicy.

RANSOM-TANSOM

Another sidewalk game that is characterized by chanting and choosing and that includes the popularity of selection and the stigma of rejection is Ransom-Tansom-Tee-I-Oh. It was popular up in Michigan in the 1930s and 1940s.

One player is chosen King and stands on the sidewalk facing perhaps four other players, who are about three sidewalk squares away. He then takes several steps toward the other players, chanting, "Here comes a king a-riding, a-riding, a-riding." Then, he stops, retreats the several steps, and chants:

Here comes a king a-riding,
Ransom-tansom-tee-I-oh.

The line of players then advances a few steps and sings back:

What are you riding here for,
Here for, here for?

They then retreat and sing:

What are you riding here for?
Ransom-tansom-tee-I-oh.

The rhyme is picked up the King:

I'm riding here to marry,

To marry, to marry.
I'm riding here to marry,
Ransom-tansom-tee-I-oh.

and then again by the line:

Who're you going to marry, marry, marry?
Who're you going to marry, ranson-tansom-tee-I-oh?

The King:

I'm going to marry the prettiest one,
The prettiest one, the prettiest one.
I'm going to marry the prettiest one,
Ransom-tansom-tee-I-oh.

The line:

Who is the prettiest one,
The prettiest one, the prettiest one?
Who is the prettiest one, ransom-tansom-tee-I-oh?

The King then gives a name, and the line asks what ransom the King is prepared to give. Often it is fantasy (jewels, wealth, fame, a throne); often it is candy, less exotic but more tangible. Then, the line huddles and decides whether they'll surrender the named member of the group for the agreed-upon ransom. Most often, the group holds out for more and chants:

Then you may not have her, have her, have her.
Then you may not have her, ransom-tansom-tee-I-oh.

And the ante escalates. Once the price is acceptable, the person joins the King as part of the royal entourage, and the game continues, with more players joining the King. Generally speaking, the popular players are always chosen first and are worth great ransoms; the less popular are also-rans. It is that kind of a game. Even when the King surprises the line by selecting either an unpopular person or one who is less pretty (called "ugly" by the line), it is recognized by the players as an act of charity.

OLD MOTHER WITCH

Also utilizing a chant and a formal structure is the Tag game Old Mother Witch. The person chosen to be "It" is the Witch. The Witch walks down the sidewalk, stooped over, as the other players walk in back of her, chanting in unison:

Old mother witch
Couldn't sew a stitch.
Picked up a penny,
And thought she was rich.

Whereupon the Witch stops and asks, "Are you there, my children?" If the group says, "No," the walk and the chant are repeated. If it says, "Yes," she turns with a screech, and the other players scatter. Whomever she touches becomes the Witch, and the game begins anew.

TAG

The simplest form of Tag is just to decide by lot who is to be "It." The other players then run off with "It" in pursuit. Whoever is touched then becomes "It." But to add zest to the game, many versions have been invented over the years, for example, a system of "safes." A safe is a haven. It can be the middle step of a stoop, a telephone pole, a bush, one particular sidewalk square marked off in chalk. Anyone being chased can make for the "safe," and as long as he stays in it or touching it, he can't be tagged.

This concept resulted in other Tag games in which a person touching a designated substance is considered safe: for example, **Iron Tag, Stone Tag, Wood Tag,** even **Squat Tag,** in which a player quickly drops into a squat to avoid being tagged.

For the daring, there is **Cross Tag,** in which a player darts between "It" and the player "It" is pursuing. "It" is then forced to chase him, and only him, until he is tagged.

Another logical extension of Tag is **Den,** in which the person who is "It" is the Hunter and those being pursued are a pack of wild beasts. Each animal has his own den: a step, a sidewalk square, a section of wall. As long as he stays there, he is safe. But if he ventures out and is tagged "caught," he then becomes part of the hunting party and helps the Hunter catch the other animals.

HIDE-AND-SEEK

Hide-and-Seek and its many forms are in a sense forms of Tag. The basic game is that the player who is "It" covers his eyes, leans forward against a wall or a tree, and counts to 100 while the others scatter and hide. At the end of the count, "It" shouts, "Ready or not, here I come," and goes to look for the others. When he discovers someone, he chases him and tags him. The player tagged then becomes "It."

In another, more difficult version, when "It" spies another player, he is permitted to race back to home base and shout, "One, two, three, I spy Jennie under the wooden porch," or whatever. The person thus caught is put "in jail" at home base. In this version, the player who is "It" has to catch every other player and, as he is doing so, keep an eye on home base because any other player can race there and free those already captured by touching them and yelling, "Home free!" In England, the game is known not only as Hide-and-Seek but also as **Lurks Off,** and it is played in exactly the same way.

A variation played in Chicago is **Tap the Icebox,** in which the person who is "It" covers his eyes and turns around while the other players stand behind him. One player draws a circle on "Its" back with his finger; then this artist or another player jabs a finger into the center of the circle, "tapping the icebox." "It" then turns and guesses who has tapped him. If his guess is right, the tapper then becomes "It" and the process is repeated. If his guess is

...27, 28, 29, 30...

wrong, he has to count to 100, eyes covered, and the rules of Hide-and-Seek apply.

In Boston, it is called **Bore a Hole.** "It" hides his eyes as the other players stand behind him chanting:

Bore a hole, bore a hole
Right through the sugar bowl.
Guess who placed the magic
Dot!

while the circle and the jab are made. "It" then turns to find all the players wagging their index fingers at him and singing, "This is the magic finger. This is the magic finger." If he guesses who the jabber was, that player becomes "It." If he doesn't, the procedure is repeated.

And in Canarsie, Brooklyn, it is **Make a Shimmalucka.** In this version, "It" hides his eyes while the circle and jab are made as someone says, "I drew a shimmalucka, and someone put his finger *in!*" At the word *in,* "It" turns and guesses. If the correct shimmalucka drawer is caught, he becomes "It." If not, it is done all over again. This particular version was noteworthy for having a "German" way of playing during World War II days. And what was "German"? Simply cheating while you were supposed to be covering your eyes.

Finally, there is the sadistic version of Hide-and-Seek played on Manhattan's Lower East Side: **Hot Peas and Butter.** "It" does not hide his eyes and count. Instead, all other players hide, and "It" hides his belt. He then summons them back, and as they hunt for the belt, eggs them on with, "You're getting hot," or "You're very cold." Whoever finds the belt is free to

114

chase—and whack—any and all other players before they reach home base. Often, the belt finder conceals his discovery and reveals it only when he has positioned himself between the players and home base. According to Jeff Morley, who still bears a few Hot Peas and Butter scars, "The pain from a belt, despite popular thinking, is not terrible, and no matter what, is short-lived."

That's what he said.

STOOPS

Miss Mary Mack Mack Mack
All dressed in black black black
With silver buttons buttons buttons
All down her back back back,
She asked her mother mother mother
For fifty cents cents cents
To see the elephants elephants elephants
Jump up the fence fence fence.
They jumped so high high high
They reached the sky sky sky,
And they didn't come back back back
Til the Fourth of July July July.

THE MOST INVENTIVE street games originated on and around stoops. Few people these days react to the word *stoop*. Many don't know, actually *don't know,* what a stoop is—was. Was it bending down? Well, yes, sort of, but also—. And when they're told that a stoop is the same as steps and stairs but always means a set of *front* stairs, there is often a quizzical, "Oh!" At any rate, *anybody* over thirty and any younger person who lives in and near a city has to know about stoops.

Stoops were everybody's playgrounds. Oh, they varied, all right. In Baltimore, they were (and are) marble; in Cleveland, they are planking. Some were brick; some, wood; some, limestone; some, brownstone. Brownstone stoops were the best, massively cut, with wide steps and rather abrupt jutting edges. They made perfect sports arenas and baseball stadia, grandstands and forums, markets and trading posts, lairs, havens, and jails. Stoops were the Himalayas as well as the Catskills, the city's front porches and the suburb's verandas, the yellow brick roads and the way to the cellar.

They were where kids sat to play the very few passive street games that existed, the core from which most active games radiated. Stoops were where we all met and sat because they were best for clapping games and card playing, for collecting movie stars' portraits and trading Topps bubble gum baseball cards, and for competitively measuring the circumferences of the silver balls we meticulously built up by collecting those little sheets of foil in cigarette packs.

Wisecracks and rhymes and our opinions on world affairs sailed off stoops, ranging from the mild:

It's raining, it's pouring
The old man is snoring
He went to bed
And bunked his head
And he couldn't get up in the morning.

to the less so:

Shoot in the pants, that's my coat he's wearing.

Popeye the sailor man
Lives in a garbage can.
He likes to go swimmin'
With bowlegged women.
He's Popeye the sailor man.

and our commentaries:

Hitler got Hungary.
He ate a piece of Turkey.
He slipped on Greece,
Broke China,
And got in Dutch.

Whistle while you work.
Hitler is a jerk.
Mussolini is a meanie,
But the Japs are worse.

Swapping anything—baseball cards, bottle tops, movie stars' pictures, collections of matchbook covers woven into accordionlike bunches, darts made of matchsticks, candy—was a prime activity of the stoops. The smarter kids always had something to trade because they would either cull magazines searching for coupons offering samples of products or write to corporations requesting such samples. Amazingly, the stoops were often well-laden with toothpastes and powders, tiny cakes of soap, and bottles and jars of all kinds of foodstuffs and face decorations. I'm told that a Lilyan Tashman picture was an even swap for a Madge Evans but that a Rudolph Valentino was traded only four-for-one for such stars as Dolores Del Rio, Marion Davies, Ralph Graves, and Ann Pennington.

Stoops were the breeding grounds for the many and mysterious clubs that sprouted in each neighborhood: the boy haters and, conversely, the girl haters, the secret handshake and signal clubs, the clubs with names like Shifter and Mischief.

A coup of one Mischief Club up in New York City's Upper West Side involved a park bench in a park named Morningside that slopes down to the Hudson River. Two members bought, legitimately, a city Parks Department bench. Then they took it to the park, put it on the grass, and sat on it—until a policeman happened along. Then, the two quite calmly picked up the bench and began walking away with it. Needless to say, the policeman chased them, asked them what they thought they were doing, and ordered them to unhand the bench. Whereupon they produced their bill of sale. It worked several times, until an injunction was gotten out that park benches thus sold were not permitted in parks. Things like that got hatched on stoops all the time.

HANGMAN

No equipment save one's spaldeen or a piece of chalk is needed for most stoop games. For instance, chalk is the sole requirement for a game like Hangman. One player is chosen, usually by "One potato, two potato," to be the Hangman; the other players are the spectators. It is the Hangman's job, of course, to hang someone and the others' to save the condemned.

The Hangman selects a word of (preferably) ten letters or more and keeps it to himself but indicates the number of letters in the word by making dashes on a stoop step. For example, if the word is *afternoon,* the Hangman chalks _____on a step. Then, each of the other players in turn has to guess a letter.

If the letter guessed is correct, say, if a player guesses *E,* then the Hangman prints that letter atop the correct dash, like this: ___*E*_____. But for each miss, a gallows and a hanged man begin to take shape with chalked lines, like this:

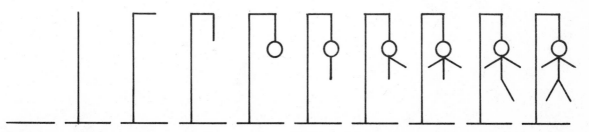

If the players fail to guess all the letters and thus the word before a complete hanged man is drawn, then the Hangman goes again. Whoever guesses the word—wild guesses are permitted—becomes the Hangman. It is a game in which a player can display his spelling ability, and there is a good deal of snobbery involved. You might encounter such dictionary-inspired Hangman words as "transmigration" or "penultimate." But if a player uses these words, he has to be prepared to define them if challenged and have his definitions checked.

DOUBLETS

A similar game is called Doublets; it also requires a sense of words and a piece of chalk. One chosen player selects two words that are totally unlike each other, perhaps opposites, but with the same number of letters. (Proper names are forbidden.) It is up to the other players to change the first word to the second, one letter at a time. The prime rule is, however, that when one letter is substituted for another, another word has to be created. It is, I suppose, a primitive form of Scrabble.

Pig, for example, can be changed to *sty* in this manner:

Pig   Pit   Sat   Sit   Say   Sty

and *poor* can become *rich* like this:

Poor   Boor   Book   Rook   Rock   Rick   Rich

Anyone is free to challenge a letter and the word it forms. A successful challenge, upheld by consulting a dictionary, permits the challenger to become the player who selects the words. An unsuccessful challenge causes the challenger to lose his turn.

PAPER ROCK SCISSORS

Paper Rock Scissors requires no chalk, only a collection of hands. It is usually played by two players at a time. Each holds a hand behind his back and at the signal "Once, twice, three, shoot!" whips out his hand, holding it either flat out with palm down (Paper), in a clenched fist (Rock), or with the first two fingers in a sort of V-for-victory position (Scissors). The rules of the game dictate that Paper covers Rock, Rock breaks Scissors, and Scissors cut Paper. The winner moves on to the next competitor in a sort of elimination contest. The player able to make his way successfully through all the other players without being covered, broken, or cut is the winner.

The rock will break the scissors.

I'M THE SALESMAN FROM ENGLAND

It is generally simpler fun to play a game such as I'm the Salesman from England, in which the player chosen as Salesman selects a color—for example, blue—and deems that it is a forbidden color and that its name cannot be spoken. He then proceeds to ask the other players questions designed to make them say the forbidden word.

I'm the salesman from England; would you like some shoes?
What color shoes would you like?
Don't you like shoes the color of the sky?
What color is the sky?
How about a sea color; you know the color of the sea, don't you?
What is it?

The answerers must always reply truthfully, although they can be evasive. Other variations include making the forbidden word *yes* or *no,* which makes for many interesting verbal contortions.

126

I'M GOING TO BOSTON

And there is I'm Going to Boston. The player chosen begins by saying, "I'm going to Boston, and I'm taking my brother." It doesn't have to be "brother"; it can be anything or any person. The next player then has to say,"I'm going to Boston, and I'm taking my brother and his fiddle." The next has to add to the verbal chain: "I'm going to Boston, and I'm taking my brother and his fiddle and my pet goat." And on it goes. If a player fails to get all the additions correct on his turn, he is out of the game and the game goes on, with the sentence getting longer and more complicated all the time. Out in the Queens section of New York City, the game is played in pig Latin and is thus a true test of tongues.

In pig Latin, for example, by the time the sentence reaches the third player, it sounds like this: "I'mgay oingay ootay ostonbay ithway ymay rotherbay nday ishay iddlefay nday ymay etpay oatgay."

Terrific.

CURSE

And then there is Curse, in which the sole object is to give another player goose bumps. This is essentially a girls' game because boys never admit that they get goose bumps, even when chalk is scraped against the school blackboards. Fingernails, even. The player designated the Witch turns another player around, and as she chants the following curse in a low voice, she illustrates the words with touches upon her prey's back:

X marks the spot
With a dot and a dot and a dash and a dash
And a big question mark.
Shiver up, shiver down
Pinch here [right shoulder], pinch here [left]
And blow where the western winds blow.

The final line is always accompanied by gentle blowing on the neck. If there are no goose bumps raised by that time, the player is considered colder than a mackerel.

TIME

A stoop game involving a whole series of guesses (or deductions, as we used to call them after watching Basil Rathbone and Nigel Bruce), is Time. This differs from most guessing games in that there is give-and-take involved; no one is "It." Usually played by a half-dozen players or more, it begins with two players going off a distance from the group and deciding on a time, perhaps 12:35 P.M. Then, they return, and the other players take turns trying to guess the time.

Whoever guesses correctly becomes a questioner and asks the two to think of and describe what *he* has been thinking of (perhaps a suit that had been bought for him). They have to use their imaginations, first, to decide what it is that is being thought of and, then, to describe it as exotically as possible. Whoever the player judges has been the most imaginative and accurate is chosen the winner, and then those two become the new time choosers.

KNUCKLES

Knuckles, or as it is more familiarly known, **Knucks,** is a game of instant pain that seems to have been designed to test the measure of one's sadism and the ability to stand pain without outward show.

Several players and a deck of cards are necessary. The game played is unimportant; it can be a simple matching game like Go Fish. What is important is not to lose—that is, not to have cards left in your hand—because the winner has the right to count the cards in each player's hand and deliver blows to the knuckles of the other players using the full deck. A player who has from one to five cards left (often the pips are counted on the cards and that decides the number) is dealt blows flat against the knuckles of his tightly clenched fist. Not too bad.

More than five means the hitter can slice the edge of the deck across the ends of the knuckles. Most times, a white scrape results; often, a bloody nick is opened. More than ten means the hitter can scrape heavily down your arm with the deck, which often opens the skin; more than fifteen means scraping the arm as well as slicing across the knuckles.

It was not at all unusual to walk into the house and when your mother asked what you had been doing, tell her, "Oh, just playing cards," even as you washed off your bloody knuckles and blotted them, hoping that your father wouldn't see them. My father always noticed *my* knuckles, and in addition to the pain on my hands, I had pain elsewhere, just for playing cards.

STOOPBALL

Stoopball is a good deal more fun. With its seemingly infinite varia-tions, it is close to being a national game. It was, and is, a one-man game, a two- or three-man game, a team game. And its devotees are in the hundreds of thousands, all believing—*knowing*—that *they* played Stoopball in the proper way.

Stoopball calls for a stoop and a spaldeen, the newer and bouncier the better. By consensus, it appears that the best stoops for Stoopball belong to brownstones. The object is to throw a spaldeen against a step and gain points or runs.

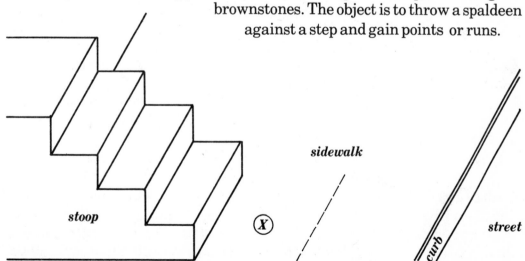

stoop   (X)   *sidewalk*   *curb*   *street*

The way you bounce the spaldeen off the stoop is important. On the West Side of Manhattan, near Central Park, a one-player version goes this way:

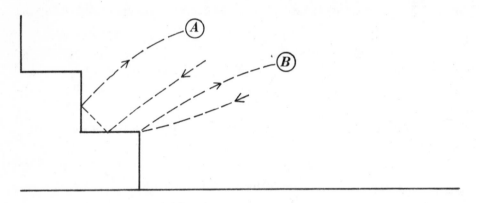

A player competes against himself. He stands in the street just behind the curb and throws the ball at the stoop. If he hits a step and then a riser (A) and catches the ball on a fly, he counts 1 point. If he throws it precisely against the point of one step (B) and catches it, he gives himself 10 points. Each time he fails to catch the ball on a fly or hit the stoop properly, he deducts 1 point, so that completing a 100-point game is quite an exercise.

The same version is played in the Bensonhurst section of Brooklyn, but with two players (one batter and one fielder) and a different method of scoring. A hit between the steps is 5 points *if* the other player does not catch the ball and 10 points if the ball goes off the point of the step and the other player does not catch it. If it is caught on the fly, the batter is out. Three outs and the

player in the field becomes the one to throw the spaldeen against the steps. It takes 100 points to win this game, too.

Over in Flatbush, yet another version flourishes.

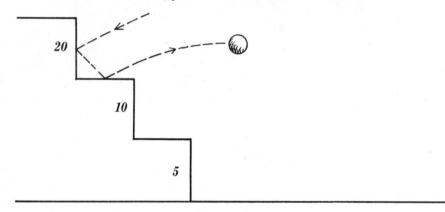

This is also for two players, and each step has its own point value. A hit on the step's point carries a bonus of 25 points. In this version, the ball is supposed to strike the riser first and then the step, the reverse of other versions. Proponents say that this method of hitting the steps creates more line drives and thus a peppier game. Again, the ball has to elude the fielder standing in the street, and it has to bounce for the points to count, the bonus 25 included. No set number of points wins, just who happens to be ahead when Mother calls you in for supper.

In still another Brooklyn version, the thrower must toss the ball and catch it himself either on the fly (10 points) or after one bounce (5 points). If he hits the edge of a step and catches the ball before it hits the ground, there is a 50-point bonus. Each player is given a certain number of throws per inning to run up his score, but if he fails to field any ball he throws, he loses the remainder of his throws for that turn. A cautious version, in which the players favor soft throws, it is often scornfully called **Sissy Ball.**

The most popular form of Stoopball is called Stoopball or **Baseball** in most parts of the United States, **Home Runs** in Brooklyn, and **Step Ball** in Philadelphia. It is a two-team form of Stoopball with three men on a team.

The batter of one team stands behind a line drawn on the sidewalk with chalk and throws the ball at the steps. What is important in these games is runs, strikes, and outs, rather than points or bonuses. In one version of Baseball, the player throws the ball either as hard or as softly as he wishes. If it bounces on the sidewalk, it is a strike. If it is caught by any of the three players on the other team, it is an out. However, if it hits the ground, every bounce increases its value as a base hit. One bounce is a single, two a double, three a triple, and four a home run. Great strategy is involved in this game as a player tries by decoy to lure fielders in close and then drive liners over their heads for bouncing home runs. Obviously, a long liner that goes over the third fielder's head is at least a four-bouncer and thus a home run. On the other hand, softly thrown balls that just clear the curb are sure singles because a fielder cannot extend his hands over the sidewalk area to catch gently dropping spaldeens.

PEACH PITS

Another night game, conceived on stoops but executed just above them, is Peach Pits. Pits of peaches are saved, dried, and squirreled away until a Peach Pit Night is called. On such a night, the pitters climb up to the fire escape above the stoop and wait, pits in hand, for the unwary. The player chosen (by "odd finger") to go first waits until people pass by and then tosses a peach pit at them. As devised by Manhattan youngsters, the point score is 20 points for a hit that strikes a couple, 5 points for a man, 3 points for a woman. The penalties are a loss of 5 points for a complete miss, going out of turn, or hitting anyone who wears glasses or carries a cane. A player loses 10 points if a person who is hit discovers where the peach pit has been thrown from.

The player collecting the most points receives a bounty of five pits from each player and the opportunity to throw first on the next Peach Pit Night. This is a game fraught with as much danger as excitement. Discovery can mean a series of instant bruises, and recognition certainly means bruises later on at home. But that doesn't stop anybody. It never has.

A missile for a summer night.

PULASKI STREET HOME RUNS

Another, more exacting game of Stoopball comes from the Bedford-Stuyvesant section of Brooklyn and involves a drawn field:

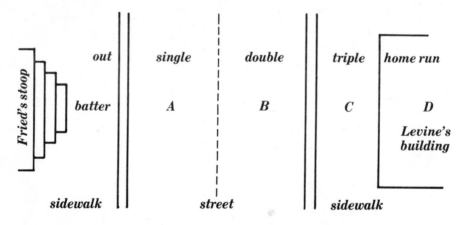

Its official name is Pulaski Street Home Runs, and the two teams usually consist of three or more players. Its rules differ from ordinary Stoopball baseball. The batter stands on the sidewalk in front of Fried's stoop and throws the ball at the steps. If it bounces on the sidewalk in front of the stoop, it is an out. Not a strike, *out*. If it bounces in the street in the area marked A (separated from B by chalk lines), it is a single, no matter how many times it bounces. If it lands in area B on one or more bounces, it is a double. To be a triple, it has to reach the sidewalk across the street on a fly; and to be a home run, it has to hit Levine's building on a fly.

This is a very tough, low-scoring game, with plently of line drives off the stoops and long fly balls caught for outs. It often is a short game because Levine sometimes takes the ball.

Philadelphia Step Ball is very much like Home Runs. A grounder off the steps into the middle of the street is a double. If a fielder handles it cleanly, it is an out; if he errs, it is a single. Like Home Runs, this is a low-scoring game that sees few base hits and even fewer homers because in West Oak, which is just outside of Philadelphia, a homer is possible only if the ball goes across the street on a fly, rolls down the slanted roof of the two-family house there, and lands safely in a drainpipe. Clearly, a very tough hit to get.

There are other variations of Stoopball, all dictated by building architecture. In New York's Harlem, for example, many of the stoops into brownstones look like this:

brownstone

stoop

curb

sidewalk

Obviously, this stoop is out of the question for any version of Stoopball. So what was devised? A game that is *called* Stoopball but that uses the groove in the retaining wall around the steps. All the rules of whatever version of Stoopball you favor are applicable. And experts are as adept at hitting the lower sharp edge of the groove as they are at hitting the point of a stoop step.

Also dictated by architecture is **Off the Wall,** a Bronx Park East game played without stoops. A batter stands a few feet away from a wall, winds up, and smashes his spaldeen underhanded against the wall, sending it zooming into the street. As in the other games, one base is scored per bounce. If the ball is caught on a fly, it is an out. Three outs to an inning, nine innings to a game.

Where the brick walls of apartment houses have concrete bases jutting out from the walls, the game of **Bumps** is in order. A ball that hits precisely where the concrete meets the bricks will bounce high into the air. This is called a "bump." A game of pop flies, with many outs and low scores. By all accounts, it is not nearly so exciting as other versions of Stoopball and certainly nowhere near as full of surprises as **Off the Point.**

There is no way of telling just how the spaldeen will fly out in Off the Point because it is thrown high against a decorative cornice of a building. These cornices, usually above the first floor of city apartment houses built in the early part of this century, are of varied shapes and styles—Greek, Romanesque, rococo, gargoyle laden, curlicued, often ugly, always interesting—and fantastic for a game that calls for quick starts and stops, changes in direction, and miraculous running and falling catches.

A cornice might look like this:

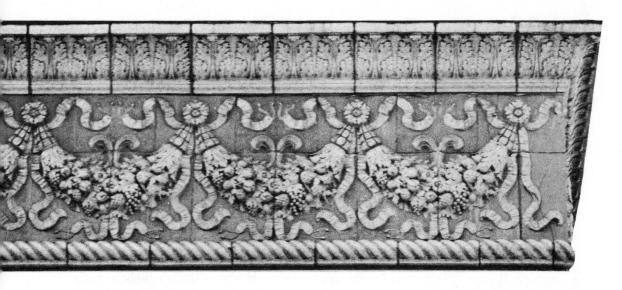

It is easy to see that a ball thrown with force against the cornice might bounce in any conceivable direction. In this game, the onus is on the thrower. He has to throw his spaldeen and catch the rebound on a fly in order to remain up. Even if he fields it cleanly on one bounce, which is something admired in other Stoopball games, he loses his turn at bat. Other pla ors will not just stand around, either, while the thrower beats himself. They have to be ready to grab the ball if the thrower muffs it, in which case the one who grabs the ball is up.

A successful catch on the fly gives the thrower 1 point, and 21 points wins. Off the Point is a game in which points are hard to come by, but it is sensational for developing reflexes.

RING-A-LEVIO

The universality of Stoopball notwithstanding, perhaps the most revered of stoop games is Ring-a-levio, an exciting Tag game, played by two teams, that might just be the most exhilarating and competitive game young girls and boys can play together. In this game (also known as **Ring-O-Levio, Ringelevio, Ringalario, Ring-O-Leary-O,** and **Ringoleavo**), one team of players hunts, captures, and jails the other team, keeping members of the hunted team imprisoned despite attempts to free them.

The two teams are chosen by two captains who choose "odds and evens" for the right to pick first; a good game has five or six players to a side. A centrally located stoop is chosen as both the Hunters' home base and as the Jail, and the Hunters go there and count to ten in unison as the other team scatters. There is no hiding because Ring-a-levio is not a Hide-and-Seek game. Instead, it is a game of agility, deception, feinting, dodging, and running, a game of staying power.

The Hunters then begin stalking, chasing, and trying to corner members of the Hunted. This game is particularly exciting in the city, where parked automobiles, fire hydrants, other stoops, and often passersby become obstacles behind which the Hunted dodge and around which the Hunters must run.

But the Hunted do get caught. When caught, a player must be held firmly as the Hunter shouts, "Ring-a-levio, 1, 2, 3!" In the Queens, New

142

The chase is on.

York, version, it's, "Caught, caught, Ring-O-Leary-O 1, 2, 3!") This done, the Hunted must stop resisting and allow himself to be taken back to the stoop and put in Jail. One member of the hunting team is then detailed to remain on guard at the Jail while the other members go back to the chase.

A player who is captured can be freed in several ways. A player from his Hunted team can race for the stoop and swipe his foot against the bottom step and shout, "Free!," whereupon the captured prisoner *must* be freed. In the Washington Heights version, a prisoner can escape on his own if he is able to jump off the stoop and avoid being tagged by the Jailer. In the Bronx, freedom is dearer; the rescuing member of the Hunted team has to race to the Jail, put his foot on a step, and shout, "Oley, Oley in free!," and still get away before the Jailer, or any member of the hunting team grabs *him* and puts him in Jail, too. Over in Brooklyn, a would-be rescuer has to do even more: run into the Jail and tag the prisoner without getting caught. If more than one prisoner is in Jail (perhaps three), they can sit together, with one of their number keeping a foot extended. If a rescuer can touch just this one prisoner, all the prisoners will be released because of their "connection" by "electricity."

Members of the Hunters are free to use the Jail as a place to rest, too, but overextended tenancy leads to scornful cries of "Base hanger," which are quite embarrassing. So quick rests are taken, and then it is back to the hunt.

Most players rely on their quickness and elusiveness to keep away from the Hunters; others depended on their strength. It is most difficult for a little guy to hold a big guy long enough to say, "Ring-a-levio 1, 2, 3. Ring-a-levio 1, 2, 3. Ringelevio 1, 2, 3!" Other players resort to trickery;

for example, if you wear your jacket loosely and unbuttoned, you can swiftly slide your arms out of it when you are grabbed, leaving the Hunter holding a waving Windbreaker.

When all members of one team are caught by the other team—truly a long process, with some chases not completed for days—then the Hunters become the Hunted. And then it begins all over again.

Ring-a-levio is one of those games that is virtually always played for a stake: sodas, candy, ice cream, often ice cream money. And the sweetest moment for the members of the victorious team is when they sit on the top steps of the stoop eating their way through two or three ice cream pops each while the losers look up longingly from the bottom of the stoop.

Dividing the captured territory.

DIRT

One bright day
In the middle of the night
Two dead boys
Got up to fight.
Back to back
They faced each other,
Then drew their swords and shot each other,
A deaf policeman
Heard the noise
And nearly killed
The two dead boys.

THE DAY OF the empty lot is over, and that is unfortunate. In the cities, there is little empty space, and what there is has been made over into parking lots and public parks. In the suburbs, housing tracts exist alongside each other, lawn hard by lawn. Unbuilt-upon land has been turned into Little League fields, golf courses, tennis courts, and fenced-in Paddle Ball arenas. And what is left is kept closed until the weekend flea markets.

Our empty lots were our Sherwood Forests, our Gettysburgs, our Bastognes, our Death Valleys, and our Bat Caves. The leafy, bushy lots were havens in which orange-crate huts sat hidden, from the trees of which dangled swings made from discarded automobile tires suspended from hemp, and in which rocks imbedded in dirt were ovens for charring marshmallows and overcooking blackened potatoes.

I grew up in a house that had a lot next to it. Throughout my youth, it was an accepted ingredient of my growing up. Only now do I realize that it was a spectacular lot. My family grew enough vegetables for the year in a part of it. In it, my father built a corrugated-tin covered shed that was a catchall combination workshop-storehouse. We had a loose brick barbecue in our lot on which we cooked in warm weather and a full-sized horseshoe court on which finger callouses were cultivated. And that was only a little part of our lot.

Our lot. That's exactly how I thought of it. Our lot. Our trees. My path. My den. And it was a shock when the bulldozers came one day and made everything level, uprooting trees and running over where I grew up. And then, they put up four houses on my lot, and I found I didn't like the houses and I didn't like the people in the houses. Furthermore, it turned out, I had to go almost a half-mile away, over near Corky's house, to find a lot that was like mine.

Lots were recognized as boys' turf. The games we played in lots, in trees, on dirt (except for the many variations of marbles into which girls were invited) were for boys. They were fighting, roughhouse games, re-creations of wars, of cops shooting robbers, cowboys attacking Indians, tests of strength and leaping and jumping in which dares and challenges and the ability to endure pain stoically were commonplace, and every-body knew girls weren't interested in that stuff. Lots were where we re-veled in newly discovered obscenities and often told the risky jokes that made us feel terribly grown up. Lots were no-girl's-land.

Games played in lots, on ground, on dirt generally are suitable only for such surfaces. It is easy to carve out a hole in the dirt with your shoe heel to create the Pot for a game of marbles. With dirt, you don't need chalk because circles and squares for marbles games can be made with the end of a twig.

MARBLES

The most popular of marbles games were played on dirt. In **Potty**, a hole is dug into the dirt with the heel. All players throw their marbles in turn at the Pot from a throwing line about seven feet away. The player whose marble is closest to the hole (if he is lucky, he will throw his marble into the Pot on the first try) goes first. He then shoots for the Pot and, once in, can use "spannies" to win other marbles; that is, he keeps any marble close enough to the Pot to fall within the distance created by stretching his thumb and forefinger. If two players' marbles are in the Pot simultaneously, each gets three chances to shoot his opponent out, which of course entitles him to the marble. This is a game of intense strategies and measurements.

Ringer, the game played each year at the National Marbles Tournament in Wildwood, New Jersey, is governed by strict playing rules.

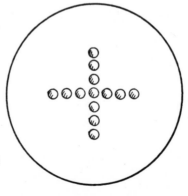

The playing circle is ten feet in diameter, and thirteen marbles are placed in an X shape in the center. When there are two players, the first one to hit seven marbles from the circle wins. As long as the winner continues to hit any marble with his shooter and knock it from the ring, he can keep on shooting (as in a run at billiards), but his shooter must stay within the circle. If it goes out of the ring, the other player shoots. This is a "for keeps" game, played for a score 7, in which the winner receives all other marbles that remain in the ring. It is "for keeps" in Queens, that is, where it is a more cutthroat game than it is in the tourney. In the national championships, the game is played for score only. Ringer has spawned many variations, but all involve the basic game of a stake of marbles at which players shot.

Old Bowler, reportedly Abraham Lincoln's specialty, is a forerunner of marble games involving a square or some other enclosure shape and involves precision shooting. The square, drawn in the dirt, looks like this:

Players have to shoot the five marbles (placed one at each corner and one in the center) off the diagram in succession, beginning with marble 1. If he fails, all marbles are replaced and the next player takes a turn. The winner usually gets a stake of marbles (or a prized shooter, an aggie, or several purees) that has been agreed upon beforehand. Today, variations of this game involving other geometric shapes are played throughout the country.

Up in Boston, a version of Old Bowler is called **Fatty Box.** In this

Abe Lincoln's marble game.

game, all players put their stakes into the square and, after choosing for "firsties," shoot. A player has to shoot a marble from the square, and his shooter has to remain in the square. If it fails to, he has to put back every marble he has already shot out. Definitely a shooter's game. Boston's version of Ringer is called, naturally, **Boston Ring** and is essentially similar to the "for keeps" game of Ringer played in Queens.

In Brooklyn's Brighton Beach, a game of marbles called **Banker Broker** is the rage of the empty lots. Little skill is involved, but the urge to gamble and the willingness to wager all on a single throw have to be quite strong. A Banker is needed, and he sets himself up in back of a hole dug into the dirt. Any player can participate simply by throwing a handfull of marbles at the hole. But before he does so, he has to say "odds" or "evens." If he chooses odds and an odd number of marbles end up in the hole, he wins an agreed-upon number of marbles. But if an even number remain in the hole, he loses them all. It is easy to see why being Banker is a good thing, and there are fights galore and various choosings before that is determined.

Similar is **Scrambooch** or **Hot Scramble,** in which all players make up a handful of marbles (mixed bags that include plain glassies, a few prized aggies, perhaps even an aggie shooter, and some valued purees) and then toss them into a patch of dirt. At a given signal—usually, "One, two, three, *shoot!*"—all players race for the area and dive into the pile of marbles, hoping to grab prizes. Definitely not a game of finesse.

A shooter's game, on the other hand, is **Spanish Pool,** also called **Dirt Pool** and **Wishing Well.** This game requires an intricate ring made up of concentric circles that looks like this:

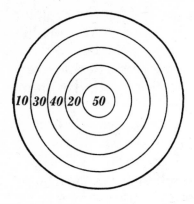

It is kind of a game of dirt darts played with marbles. Players shoot for score and for whatever stake has been agreed upon. From the placement of the point values on the rings, it is easy to see why precision in shooting is a prerequisite. Each player receives a specified number of chances from a predetermined shooting spot, and the one with the highest score is obviously the winner.

An intricate shooting-gambling game native to rural Minnesota utilizes the familiar heel-dug holes. It is called **Pots** and requires nine of them to be dug. The holes are placed rather close together, and some fancy shooting is required. Each player puts a number of marbles into the center pot, which is slightly larger than the others. This becomes the Bank. Then, each shoots at the smaller holes, marked "win" or "lose." Getting into a winning pot allows a player to withdraw a specified number of marbles from the Bank. Going into a losing pot carries with it a marbles penalty.

154

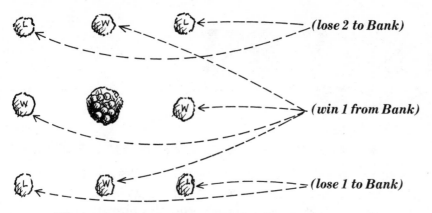

(lose 2 to Bank)

(win 1 from Bank)

(lose 1 to Bank)

The game continues until the Bank is empty. Rather a lengthy game, one of those all-afternoon things interrupted only by mothers when they call everybody in for supper.

In the Brownsville section of Brooklyn and on the Lower East Side of Manhattan, a marbles game played with nuts and called **Passover** thrives.

Either two hazelnuts or two filberts are declared the stake and placed in a hole (the Pot) dug in the narrow strip of dirt between sidewalk and curb. Other hazelnuts are used as shooters and are either looped toward the Pot, basketball-fashion, or shot toward the Pot off the thumb with the forefinger. If your nut goes into the Pot, you win the nuts, an after-supper snack.

JOHNNY ON A PONY

For example, Johnny on a Pony, a game for strong backs and legs, is out-of-bounds to girls. In this game, there are two teams, usually of five or six boys each. The first team is the Pony, and the second is Johnny. The Pony team lines up this way: One member stands upright with his back braced against a tree; then the second player bends down, thrusts his head into the first person's stomach, and grabs him tightly around the waist. The next bends down, placing his head between the legs of player 2 and grabbing him tightly around the thighs. Players 4, 5, and 6 repeat what number 3 did. The whole team then braces.

The Johnny team, which tries to enlist all the heavy kids in the neighborhood, races at them, one at a time, and vaults atop the row of backs as far forward as he can, shouting, "Johnny on a Pony, one, two, three!" The heaviest member of the team is saved for last because the object is to cave in the backs of the braced Pony team. If the jumping team can do that, the others must brace themselves again for another onslaught. If they hold and support all six members of the other team, then that team becomes the Pony and the jumpers have to bend over. Sprained backs and cricks in the neck characterize Johnny on a Pony, which in Philadelphia and the Bronx is called **Buck Buck.**

The game is the source of several imitations and variations. **Leap Frog,** in which boys take turns bending over to permit others to vault over their backs and in which they then become vaulters, is derived from Johnny. In parts of England, Leap Frog is called **Buck Jumping;** and in Saint Louis, it is **Bumbay.** A two-man, two-team version of Johnny called **Rum Stick a Bum** was played in Nottingham, England, in the early part of this century.

A New York version is **Pile On,** in which one person is the prey. He leans over, grabbing tightly either to a fire hydrant or to several fence pickets, and then tries to stay up as successive playmates jump onto his back. He stays as long as he can and is replaced by the player under whose weight he finally collapses.

And an even-rougher version that adds an element of chance is played in Boston and is called **Billy Billy Buck.** Here, the fellow leaning over is leaped upon by the first player, who, after landing and sitting, holds up one, two, or three fingers and shouts, "Billy Billy Buck, how many fingers do I have up? One, two, three, or none?" If the player bent over guesses correctly, the one astride him then becomes "It." If he guesses wrong, the first player on stays on, another player vaults astride, and the guessing continues. If it happens to be "Its" unlucky day, he will probably collapse under the weight of a bunch of his fellows; after the collapse, he becomes "It" again. A not-nice, no-quarter game.

INDIAN GAMES

Less violent and more challenging are Indian-style games, the first requirement for which are trails, which were literally worn-smooth footpaths through lots and dense brush that are given names just as surely as streets and avenues are. Playmates arrange to meet at one end or another of certain trails and set off from there on games such as **Hare and Hounds.**

One person is dubbed the Hare in this game and given a package of chalk. He sets off through the trails, to be followed after a suitable time by the Hounds. The Hare makes tiny chalk marks on rocks, under broken limbs, on tree trunks, on scrap, whatever, or else he drops shards of chalk as he goes, leaving a trail for the Hounds to follow. The first Hound to spot the Hare is the winner.

A more complex version of this, called **Follow the Arrow,** is played in Washington, D.C. Two teams, usually of two or three players each, compete. One is the prey; one, the hunter. Those being hunted lead off and every twenty or thirty feet draw an arrow to denote the direction in which they are going. Great pains are taken to be honest, and if an arrow is marked on a tree trunk pointing upward, for example, it is generally assumed that a person is either up the tree or did climb up so that an arrow could honestly have been placed there. When the team being hunted decides to stop running, it makes a set of arrows that looks like this:

$$\begin{array}{c} \uparrow \\ \leftarrow \bigcirc \rightarrow \\ \downarrow \end{array}$$

These arrows tell the pursuers that the prey is holed up in the vicinity, usually about 100 feet or so in any direction. The fun is in finding well-hidden arrows along the route. They can be drawn on the undersides of rocks, on leaves, on twigs, in the dirt, anywhere at all. Like most good and inventive games, it requires no equipment. And even if nobody has chalk, a piece of coal can be swiped, or a quartzy rock can be used to scrape the trail of arrows.

MUMBLETY-PEG

On my block, dirt was associated with knives. A knife was as necessary to one's image as trousers, and there was really only one kind: The Boy Scout knife. Oh, there were boys who had small mother-of-pearl-handled knives that shone brightly and whittled fairly well, but for games in the dirt, there was really no substitute for the Boy Scout knife. Today, I expect a Swiss army knife has equal status, but on my block, we didn't know about Swiss armies. A paring knife wouldn't do, nor any other sort of kitchen knife, nothing but a Boy Scout knife, with its rough buffalo horn handle and all those spoons, forks, bottle openers, can openers, screwdrivers, and things that folded into them. We never used any of these utensils, but it denoted status to have them. Knife games in the dirt were, and are, popular. They can be as simple or as complicated as you might wish.

The best-known knife game is Mumblety-Peg, or as we all called it **Mumbledy-Peg** or **Mumbly-Peg.** Necessary equipment? Dirt, Boy Scout knife, and a deft hand.

Mumblety-Peg is designed to test and demonstrate skill in knife sticking. By the way, the use of an ice pick is permitted where it is known that a player is not too expert a sticker, but generally ice picks are frowned upon.

First, toss the knife by the blade end over end into the dirt so that it sticks, blade down. Then, hold the knife point on a fingertip and flip it outward, sending it toward the ground. Each time the blade sticks, the player

Off the finger is easy . . .

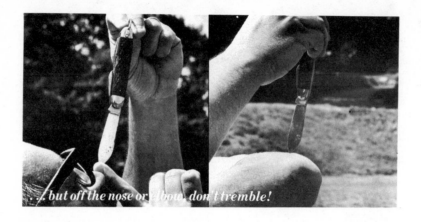

... but off the nose or elbow, don't tremble!

goes on to the next step: a progression of knife flips that go (depending upon the neighborhood or agreed-upon rules) from the tip of the nose, to the chin, to the shoulder, to the elbow, to the hip, to the knee, and finally off the tip of the sneaker. The first competitor to run the course successfully has the right to drive a peg (we used a matchstick) into the dirt with three blows of the knife handle, and the loser has to bury his face in the dirt and pull the peg out with his teeth.

Mumblety-Peg is also called **Stick In** because of the loser's obligation.

Opinions on technique in Mumblety-Peg differ. The first shot, in which the knife is tossed swiftly downward end over end is rather straightforward. But depending upon a player's height, ability to bend, and relative strength and skill, the force and number of flips for all of the other fancy shots varies. There really is no right way to throw a Mumblety-Peg knife. It's simply thrown.

TERRITORY

A knife game that requires true throwing skill is Territory. This is best played by three players, who, by choosing, become countries. Germany was definitely a bad country to be when I was growing up, and so was Japan. America was good; France was okay; Great Britain was next. A diagram is drawn in the dirt and divided equally among the countries, like this:

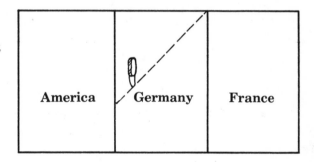

The player who is America goes first. He attacks Germany by tossing his knife into that territory, and whichever way the blade sticks becomes the path for a line extended across the country. Once divided, Germany is asked which part of the country he wants. And as long as America keeps slicing (after successfully sticking) Germany can continue to be carved up. A country remains alive as long as the player representing it can hold two fingers flat down in his country. If he can't, the entire country is lost. As often happens, once Germany is out of business, Allies begin attacking each other. Oh, well.

BLIND MAN'S BLUFF

Lots are fine for such games as **Blind Man's Buff,** which most of us have always called Blind Man's Bluff. One fellow, "It," chosen by "odd-finger," is blindfolded, usually with a scarf or a long stocking. He is then surrounded by the other players and spun around by the shoulders repeatedly until he is reeling about dizzily. He then has to follow the sounds of people walking, urgings-on by the other players, teasings, duckings, shovings, until he touches another player, which he tries to do with desperate lungings. The one touched then becomes the Blind Man.

A 1930s suburban New York version called **Grunt, Pig, Grunt** also involves a blindfolded player ("It") surrounded by the other players grouped in a circle. The blindfolded player gropes around the circle, finally pointing his finger at one player and commanding, "Grunt, Pig, Grunt!" The person pointed at has to squeal and grunt and snort like a pig (or at least the way he *thinks* a pig might squeal and grunt and snort), and "It" tries to guess his name. If he guesses correctly, the person named is blindfolded and goes through the same process. This game is not recommended for cities, particularly for areas that might be within hearing distance of a police station.

WEAPONS

Empty lots are fine places for games such as **Robin Hood** and the various forms of **Guns,** both games of incipient violence. Robin Hood is a rather basic game. One player makes a bow out of a thick sapling branch and taut cord and some arrows out of straight-as-possible sticks and then runs after the other players, shooting the arrows at them. This is not as dangerous as it might seem because there is usually very little pull in the homemade bows and the arrows are covered at one end with globs of clay and usually fail to fly truly. But the game is fun anyway.

Guns is played with store-bought lead guns, or homemade ones. One kind is made by taking a length of board, hammering a large nail on one side to make a grip, and holding a smaller piece of wood against the first by means of a thick length of inner tube. It looked like this:

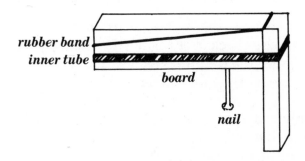

rubber band

inner tube

board

nail

A player holds the gun by gripping the piece of wood and the nail and making a fist. Inward pressure tips the top of the piece of wood away from the board, and the rubber band, wedged between the two pieces of wood, flies out. Rubber bands are the bullets. If a player is hit by one, he is considered dead and eliminated from the game.

Another type of gun is made from the corner of a Sunkist orange crate by cutting off portions of the notched corner, leaving a wooden triangle which becomes the trigger. It looks like this:

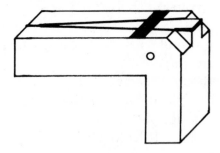

A nail is driven through the joint to keep it firm. A rubber band is nailed to the front and stretched back over the notch. Then, a paper clip is pushed into the stretched band, and the gun is loaded. This gun is held in a fist, and the thumb is used to ease the taut rubber band over the end of the notch, whereupon the paper clip is sent flying. Paper clips are dangerous to shoot out and so were frowned upon. Besides, they are hard to get. So, tightly folded pieces of paper or stiff cardboard are used as bullets instead. The same rules apply. Hit is dead, and dead is out.

MORE TAG

Empty lots are fine for such Tag games as **Wood Tag,** in which "It" cannot tag any other players so long as they touch wood, because wood abounds in lots. And there is **Shadow Tag,** a sunny-day test in which "It" has to run after the other players and, instead of tagging them, touch their shadows with his foot. A fast, exciting game that has more than its share of arguments.

And so is **Freeze and Melt.** "It" stands in the center of a circle of other players, who move, wheel about, and advance on "It" until he yells, "Freeze!" Then, they have to stop exactly where they are and in position, not moving anything except their eyes. Blinking is accepted. If "It" detects someone moving—after all there are players behind him, and some try to sneak a move—he points him out, and that is the signal for all other players to pummel the mover.

If "It" does not detect a move, he can permit the frozen to move again by shouting, "Melt!" Then, the process is repeated. However, "It" can have the tables turned on him. If, while the group is frozen, he fails to see someone behind him move and that person succeeds in touching "It," all the other players close in on "It" and pummel *him.*

Once "It" is touched, he almost always gets beaten because he invariably spins to see who has touched him, and then someone else touches him, and the lynching is on. Nice.

ROUGHHOUSING

An activity that is both a game and a means of settling disputes is **Back Fights,** in which opposing teams of two each fight each other knight-style. One player gets on another's shoulders and runs at another pair of players similarly set up. There is much pushing, shoving, and a fair amount of punching, and it is incumbent upon both the rider and the horse to maintain balance. The jousts are more fun when they aren't over some point of contention because then the players aren't so bent on destroying each other as they were in playing King Arthur and the Round Table, with all sorts of made-up-on-the-fly tournament and jousting rules. But like other games that boys feel obliged to take part in, it is one you can get hurt playing.

Hurts of a less intentional nature occurred in a fast, tough game played in the 1930s in the east end of Toronto, Canada. It was a game invented on the spot, created by a curious set of circumstances, as so often happens with childhood games. A group of rather well-to-do young men in Toronto, Montreal, Buffalo, and Rochester formed a polo league; in Toronto, they played at the Woodbine Race Track. Toronto youngsters hung around the track and did such things as watering and walking the polo horses, keeping score of goals by waving red flags, and running messages. The youngsters were paid from twenty-five cents to a dollar, no mean salary in those depression days, but an additional benefit was that they were given the used polo equipment.

168

Polo mallets, made of solid wood and set on bamboo poles, were splintered, discarded, and given to the boys. The wooden balls, once brightly painted, were likewise discarded after they had been knocked about and discolored with use. These, too, were collected by the youngsters. Often, the balls were repainted. The mallets were cut down, the splintered portions taken out of the holes in mallet heads, and the shortened poles then reinserted into the heads. Thus equipped, the youngsters played **Polo** in vacant lots, pretending they had horses, running, and swiping through the grass in what surely is unique among the games of modern children. There were sprains and bruises and black-and-blue blotches on arms, legs, and ankles; but by all accounts, the youngsters had enormous fun.

Saluggi, or **Saloogie**, is another rather simple game that derives from torment. Two or more players simply take something (a barrette, a small doll, a penknife, a prized ball, a comb, virtually anything that can be construed as somewhat of a treasure) from another kid and throw it back and forth, dashing up and down the sidewalk while the owner tries desperately to get back his or her property.

The only rules are that whoever catches the item must shout, "Saloogie on Chris's knife!," or "Saloogie on Stevie's model plane!," or whatever and that the victim must be angry, which is not at all difficult. It is not necessary to choose up for a game of Saloogie; rather, the predators have to decide on a victim, which is also not difficult.

BUCKEYES

Not at all unique is a game common to suburban children and to those kids fortunate enough to live in the neighborhood of horse chestnut trees. It utilizes the chestnut (often called a *buckeye*) and string, persistence, and the ability to withstand instant sharp pain and is, by all accounts, immensely rewarding. It is known as **Buckeyes** or **Victories** or **Chestnut Killers,** depending upon whether the players live in Pittsburgh or Brooklyn.

The game is simple enough. You wait until late September, after the horse chestnuts have fallen from the trees, after their bumpy, spiny covering has dried out and is removable, and after they have almost completely dried out, too. The horse chestnut, or buckeye, is selected carefully for its shape. The best are round and slightly flattened at both poles.

A hole is carefully made, preferably with a thin nail, through the middle, and string is pushed through and knotted. The chestnut is then pressed down into the knot, and the buckeye or killer is born.

There are several ways of holding your chestnut, such as:

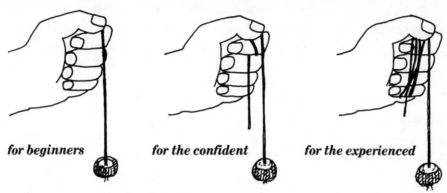

for beginners　　　　*for the confident*　　　　*for the experienced*

One player holds his chestnut suspended, not moving his hand, while the other twirls his around, swings it, gathers speed, and smashes it against the first nut. Generally, the player doing the hitting swings the chestnut over a shoulder and back, counting "one and two," and then yells "Strike!" At that point, he hits the other nut. If he hits it but does not break it, he gets another turn. If he misses the chestnut altogether, the other player has a turn to hit *his* buckeye.

In Pittsburgh, once a player succeeds in breaking another's chestnut, he is considered King. For each successive victory, he acquires another level. Thus, he can become King 2 with another breaking, then King 3, and so on. Because there are buckeye tourneys all over the place, it is possible for classic showdowns (say, a King 12 challenging a King 14), and whoever wins has the right to claim the combined total as part of his title, thus becoming, in this instance, King 26.

In Brooklyn, a winner was a Killer not a King. With each victory, he is considered a 2-Killer, 3-Killer, and so forth. By late October, when the horse chestnuts have hardened unbelievably, the player who has had the sense to put aside a stock of nuts early, preparing them for combat while they are still green, will emerge the ultimate winner, perhaps a 150-Killer or a King 200.

There is a whole method of preparation that good players take the time to adhere to. Once the nut is picked and the outer covering removed, you polish the nut carefully, getting off every bit of the residue from the covering. A nail is driven through the still-soft meat, and then the nuts are placed in vinegar to hasten the hardening process. Once removed from the vinegar, the spare nuts are strung onto a thick string or, more preferably, a shoelace, like this:

Players are expected to tell the truth about the number of victories they have achieved, and honesty is assumed, except, for example, when a fellow claims to be a 15-Killer and his chestnut is new and undented. Once someone loses and has his chestnut smashed, he has to begin again from the bottom.

There are variations of this game. In Yonkers, a New York suburb, for example, it is not enough to crack your opponent's chestnut to win. It has to be demolished and fall crumbling to the ground. Another Yonkers ploy is to swing the killer so that the two strings intertwine, and then the person who is attacking has the right to yank down on the string. If the other player's nut falls to the ground, the player can yell, "Stomp!," or "Stompies!," and jump on the chestnut, virtually assuring victory. However, that is a game of considerably less finesse and is frowned upon by chestnut purists.

WILL-O'-THE-WISP

One of the few dirt and lot games that depends on one's honor is Will-o'-the-Wisp. Most times you have to have witnesses to see that a player's word is kept, to see that there is no cheating. And this game offers one of the best ways to do it in the lots. It is essentially a Hide-and-Seek game but is played only at dusk as the light gets bad. The one who is "It" searches through the darkened bushes and weeds and behind trees looking for prey. When he is found, "It" tags him, brings him back to base, and calls the other players in for the night with "Allee alee in free!" The one caught is then recognized as "It" for whatever game begins the new day tomorrow. He is known to be "first by day."

CURBS

All the girls in France
Do the hula-hula dance,
And the way they shake
Is enough to kill a snake.
When the snake is dead,
They put flowers in his head.
When the flowers die,
They put diamonds in his eyes.
When the diamonds break,
It is 1948.

Freeze!

GUTTER HAS COME to mean something nasty these days, but most of us who were kids a few years back remember gutters with a certain fondness. A gutter was a street between two curbs—not a descriptive word for foulness or for those copper, wood, and lately, vinyl troughs that drain water gently off suburban roofs—just a street. When you told your mother you would be out playing in the gutter until she wanted you in for the night, all she said was, "Watch out for the cars."

And you had to. Often, the fluidity of One-on-One basketball ebbing and flowing in the gutter underneath the homemade potato-bushel hoop hammered into a telephone pole was abruptly halted with "Time!" or "Fins!" to let cars pass through the court. Neighborhood-dare stickball games, the results of one block challenging another, were halted in midswing, it often seemed, to allow delivery trucks through.

But that was all right because passing vehicles themselves were a sort of fun in the gutter. You could stick out your tongue at the drivers or— terrific psychological satisfaction—get out of the car's way in excessive slow motion, forcing the driver to slow down, shift gears, perhaps even stop, as you nonchalanted yourself out of midstreet. You could have (as we often did) handfuls of shredded leaves in your pocket, ready to be thrown at a car windshield to make the driver think for an instant that scores of pebbles and rocks were heading toward him. That fleeting look of concern on his face was instant gratification, and if he got out of his car in anger to chase us— Heaven!

But these were transitory pleasures, fringe benefits. The games lasted for hours. Streets were where we played those games that required vaster space than that afforded by sidewalks and stoops and in places where there were no empty lots. They became one- and two-manhole-cover-long football gridirons and baseball fields, where long hits were what counted, not just the number of bounces of a spaldeen. Gutters were for dodging and feinting, for end sweeps, for lining up for five-man rushes. They were wide rivers and valleys that had to be either navigated or trekked across from the safety of one sidewalk to the other.

Jump ropes flew higher and were less confined in the gutter. Curbs were foul lines, boundaries, and benches on which pinch hitters waited with impatience. What was better than a street on which to echo the clattering of Kick the Can? Can a game like Punchball be played anywhere but in a gutter? Today, the streets are still important playgrounds (more so in the cities than in the suburbs), and many, many sidewalk-to-sidewalk games are playable only in streets, no matter where.

BASKETBALL

In cities in general and New York City in particular, the gutter was the only basketball court most of us ever knew. Today, with the enormous growth of professional basketball and the wide interest in it, there isn't a park or recreation area of any size that doesn't have a basketball court or two crammed into it. This was not always so, nor is it completely so yet. The streets are still basketball courts for thousands of black and Hispanic youngsters in New York, many of whom see proficiency in basketball as a ticket out of the ghetto. This has proved to be the case for many of the finest basketball players now in the professional leagues. Black stars dominate the game and have conferred upon it a style recognized as eastern or New York basketball, which in its simplest terms is head to head, one on one, me against you. Nor is the eastern influence on basketball a new phenomenon; it's just different. In its early days, eastern or New York basketball was Jewish basketball, a game of the streets, a game of speed, fast passing, and teamwork.

Street basketball in all of its forms is composed of equal portions of skill and guile. Its best players are either those who are masters of moving and weaving the basketball toward the net by passing and dribbling or those who have the touch to shoot—and score—from any part of the court. It was played against a backboard slapped together from discarded planks on which was hung anything that would serve as a hoop, and it was learned

Basketball—the city game.

only in the streets. It still is.

Al Cruz, a student of New York basketball and a teacher of it in the city's Department of Parks and Recreation for more than twenty years has seen the face of the game change. "The white kids had more ego involved," he says. "They fought more, they got more angry because the contact in the game got to them and they would argue heatedly over fouls. The black kids find more fun in it, I think. They accept the banging and the jostling under the boards. That action is okay. The feeling is they'll take anything to get off their shot.

"It's really a black game, a minority game, now. The blacks are playing basketball and the whites are playing touch football." What's more, a great many Spanish-speaking kids are playing street basketball these days, too, because, he says, "they're getting heavier. They're six feet, six-two and heavier and can get into the flow of the board action." Whether a different style of play will emerge remains to be seen.

The most common form of street basketball usually has three or four players to a side, and play takes in one full court. In the gutter, a full court extends from curb to curb, with other boundaries marked off with chalk; a manhole cover designates both the keyhole and the foul-shooting area. It generally looks like this:

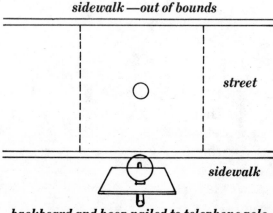

sidewalk —out of bounds

street

sidewalk

backboard and hoop nailed to telephone pole

The team with the ball (chosen with the flip of a coin or by "odds-and-evens") takes the ball into the court from the far curb, and play begins. All the rules of basketball apply, and if the luxury of a referee is available, fouls are called. The one difference is that after a successful foul shot, the team given the ball must take it back into the court again from the far curb. There is no point limit in this game. Whoever has the most points at suppertime wins.

The game acquires juice and spice when there is no referee and players call their own fouls. Arguments—many and loud—usually ensue unless it is agreed beforehand that any foul disputes are settled by choosing.

A favorite common gutter basketball game is **One-on-One.** It can be played full court across the width of a street, but it is generally confined to one-half of the street, from the manhole cover to the curb where the basket hangs. In most of these games, a player can shoot from anywhere, anytime, and anyhow he pleases. If the shot fails to go in, he may drive in for his own rebound and lay it up in an attempt to score. In other versions, he may not compete for the rebound; instead, the other player must pick it off and take it behind the manhole-cover foul area and then bring it in. This game, too, is played with or without fouls.

In One-on-One, all baskets (field shots, lay-ups, and fouls) count 1 point each, and 21 points wins the game. However, a player must win by 2 points.

Another game, **Scuttlebutt,** is best played by three players. Two players defend against one, yet each player has his own score. No fouls are called in this game, but the defending players have the right to call walking, double dribbling, and self-passing as infractions, thereby causing the offending player to lose the ball. A basket scored from the field is 2 points; one from in front of the foul line is 1.

When one player reaches 11 points (halfway to the winning total of 21), any player who does not have at least 3 points must go to the bench. A player must also score exactly 21 points to win. Scoring 22 with a long shot (the result of either miscounting your own score or shooting from a 2 zone when you thought you were in a 1 zone) automatically sends the shooter back to 13. A good competitive game, with more emphasis on field moves because of the two defenders.

Another variation is **Twenty-one,** and the emphasis here is on the foul-shooting abilities of the two players. The first player steps to the foul line and begins shooting fouls; each one counts 2 points. He continues shooting for as long as he succeeds in sinking the ball through the hoop. The opposing player stands beneath the hoop; if a foul shot should miss, he has the opportunity to grab the rebound and toss in a lay-up. If he is successful, he receives 1 point and moves to the foul line to shoot while the first player moves under the basket. Again, the winning score is 21, and it must be scored exactly. For example, a player with 20 points will deliberately miss a foul shot so that he can stand under the boards, hoping his opponent misses a foul so that he can take a lay-up for the winning point. If a player goes over 21 with a shot, he goes back to 0 and begins again.

Expert foul shooting is the key to winning another street basketball game that can be played by as many as care to. It is called **Fouls.** Each player has the opportunity to shoot the ball twenty-one consecutive times from the foul line; each basket counts 1 point. The one with the highest score after each player has taken his shots is the winner. This game is notable for the whammies and heckling each shooter is subjected to as he tries to deep-breathe his way to full concentration for his foul shooting. Players without some sort of a touch are discouraged from participating in Fouls, which is always played for ice cream money or other stakes.

Horse, a highly competitive game, is kind of a basketball adaptation of **Follow-the-Leader.** It is for two players only, and a distinct advantage belongs to the player who goes first. A player with, say, a fantastic half-court left-handed jump shot dribbles about anywhere he wishes on the court until he gets to "his" spot; then, he makes his move, turns, and takes his favorite shot. If it goes in, the other player is obliged to dribble, move, and shoot in exactly the same way—and to score.

If he misses, he is awarded the letter h. Then, the first player undoubtedly takes the same shot again and tosses the ball to his opponent. Each miss carries with it a letter, until H - O - R - S - E is spelled out; the first player earning the word is declared the loser.

A game in which the emphasis is on ball handling is **Dribble,** often called **Steal the Dribble.** There is absolutely no shooting involved. One player stands in the foul-shooting area and begins dribbling as if he is about to drive on the basket for a lay-up. It is up to the opposing player to force him to fumble the ball, to discontinue dribbling, to double dribble, any of which is grounds for losing the ball. If the dribbler does err, his opponent gets 1 point and possession of the ball and then must attempt the dribble. On the other hand, a dribbler can earn 1 point if he breaks through the defense and clearly has a shot on basket if he wishes to. A game for the deft, for those wishing to polish their skills, for shooters who can do it all and now want to become Walt Fraziers.

Wall Ball—fast ball pitching only.

STICKBALL

A game synonymous with streets, city streets in particular, is Stickball, a baseball-oriented game that to its players and fans is major league all the way. Unlike most unorganized and pickup baseball and softball games, which generally consist of a bunch of kids getting together for an hour or so of competitive run scoring, Stickball is, to its artful practitioners, both fun and serious business. Hitters practice their swings continuously, and pitchers pitch by the hour to strike zones chalked on walls or to gutter home plates, perfecting motion and delivery.

A hitter who can consistently rocket a spaldeen more than two sewers straight down a gutter receives as much neighborhood adulation as did say, major leaguers Joe DiMaggio and Willie Mays (who, it must be said, was a legendary city-street slugger, always a three- or four-sewer hitter). A pitcher who can squeeze and knuckle a spaldeen so that when he pitches on a bounce to a hitter—who is waiting with his sawed-off broomstick bat cocked behind his ear—the ball careens crazily off to one side or another or bounces back with such backspin that it appears to be on a leash is regarded as akin to Sandy Koufax.

Stickball is the national game of American cities, played by city children who cannot afford the caps and gloves and hard balls and mitts and bats and catchers' masks needed for full-fledged baseball or have the luxury of large unbuilt-upon expanses of dirt on which to lay out baseball diamonds with bases.

Stickball is city baseball. Manhole covers are home plate and second base. A telephone pole might be first base; a fire hydrant, third. Any combination of urban fixtures that can be roughly construed to resemble a diamond is a suitable playing field. Often, a rear fender of a parked car is a base, and a first baseman reaching his foot back and up onto a fender while his hands stretch to catch a belly-high ball thrown by the shortstop is sheer ballet.

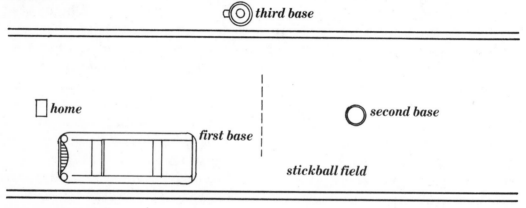

third base

home

first base

second base

stickball field

The pitcher's mound is generally a chalked line in the middle of the gutter, behind which the pitcher has to stay when making the swooping, half-sidearm, half-underhand pitch that is characteristic of most good Stickball pitchers. A word about the ball: A spaldeen is always preferred, but in a pinch, a tennis ball with good bounce and with its fuzz completely rubbed off will do nicely.

186

There are many varieties of Stickball, the most common being **Pitching In,** in which there are as many as five players on a side. If there are six, then each team will have its own catcher; if not, then one member of the batting team catches.

The pitcher delivers the ball on one bounce, and the batter swings. A miss is a strike, and two strikes are an out. If he hits the ball, all baseball rules apply. He runs to first, second, and third and can be thrown out on a ground ball. If the ball is a fly and is caught, he is out.

The one exception, dictated by urban geography, is that any ball (no matter how well hit, no matter how long) that goes over a fence or a hedge that is around property lived on by people the players hate is an automatic out—and the batter has to go get the ball. This kind of thing often spices up the game.

There are usually two outs per side per inning, and games are customarily seven innings long. It is not at all unusual to have no-hitters pitched if a pitcher is "on" that day. A tougher form of this is **Twilight,** played at dusk with extra-fast pitching decreed.

A variation of this form of Stickball is called **Long Stick,** in which there is no pitcher. The batter tosses the ball upward, grabs his bat and either hits the ball before it hits the ground or misses. All other Stickball rules apply. Hardly a scientific game, although truly fine hitters have field days with Long Stick.

A third form of the game, which everyone knows by the name of **Wall Ball** or **Wall Stickball,** is usually for two players: a batter and a pitcher. A strike zone is drawn on a wall, and the batter stands next to it, awaiting the pitches thrown into it on a fly.

Stickball, where three sewers is deep center fi[eld]

If the ball hits within the strike zone and the batter doesn't swing or swings and misses, it is an out. If he foul-tips the ball, it is a strike. Two strikes to an out, three outs to an inning. A ground ball hit by the batter and fielded cleanly by the pitcher is an out, too. If he errs on the grounder, it is a single. If the ball is hit past the pitcher, a base is added for each bounce. One bounce is a single; two, a double; three, a triple; four, a homer. Obviously, any ball hit sharply past the pitcher is a home run.

When the batter faces another building, which is rather common, a ball hit on or just above the second floor is generally a double; above the third floor, a triple; above that or on a roof, a home run. This version of Stickball is usually a head-to-head game between the best hitter and the best pitcher, usually for a stake, and with a large audience in attendance.

Another Stickball game is **Rotation,** a game to be played when many kids aren't around and planned so that everybody gets a shot at all phases of the game. Also called **One-O-Cat** and **Cat and Dog** (in Pittsburgh), it is played by three players: a batter, a short-fielder, and an outfielder.

The batter throws the ball up and hits it. He is allowed two swings. A ball hit past the short-fielder is a single; past a chalked line, a double; past some landmark, a triple; and past the outfielder, a homer. Two outs are permitted per inning, and when the batter makes two outs, the short-fielder becomes the batter, the outfielder moves to the short field, and the batter moves to the outfield. A good competitive time passer of a game.

Another fine three-player Stickball game is **Tag Ups.** In this game, there is only one fielder, a batter, and a runner who stands on third base. The batter hits a fly ball (only fly balls are permitted), and at the moment the fielder catches it, the man on third base races for home. The batter then becomes the catcher and is responsible for tagging the runner out. Each time the runner scores, a run is counted for him; each time he is tagged, he is out. There are two outs to an inning, and after two outs are made, the players rotate, with the runner on third becoming the batter, the batter becoming the fielder, and the fielder going to third base. This is an interesting variation and possibly the only Stickball game in which the emphasis is on neither the batting nor the pitching.

A variation of Rotation is **Flies Up,** in which the rotation can be upset if a fly ball is caught by either the short-fielder or the outfielder. If, for example, the outfielder catches the ball on a fly, he becomes the batter, the batter takes his place, and the short-fielder remains in position.

Although Stickball is important in New York City, it has become so diversified that it is called many things in many parts of the city. It can be **Twilight** in East Harlem; **Pot Ball** out near Rockaway Beach, where a long-handled discarded kitchen pot replaces the broomstick; and **Flatbush** out in Brooklyn, where the broomstick is in order and a soft sponge-rubber ball is used instead of a spaldeen.

In Philadelphia, **Indian Ball** is played. The batter hits by himself, then places the broomstick across whatever has been designated home plate. Whichever fielder of three or more retrieves the ball rolls it at the bat. If it hits and the batter catches it as it bounces up, he remains at bat. If he does not catch it, or if he drops it, whoever rolled the ball becomes the batter.

And there does come a time when your spaldeen splits—a calamity, but not a dire one because then you can play **Egg Ball,** a Brooklyn game of chance rather than skill, featuring either no runs or floods of runs, all dependent upon the "egg", which is one half of a spaldeen. The ball is pitched and, when hit, flops about. No line drives are possible, and the egg barely makes it past the pitcher's mound, but it is a chore to catch the ball cleanly. A crazy game, played only when there is absolutely nothing else to do and when pooled money cannot make up the twenty cents needed for a new spaldeen.

In parts of Pennsylvania, this game is called **Half Ball.** When even a half spaldeen isn't available, a four-inch length of garden hose is used, in which case the game is called, naturally, **Hose Ball.** And up in Boston, they use either a length of hose or a chunk of bicycle tire for a baseball-type game called, oddly, **Kick the Bar.** The tire is stood on end at home plate and kicked by the batter. It is fielded and then thrown, not *to* a baseman to retire the batter-kicker, but *at* the batter as he is running to base. If he is hit, he is out—and often hurt.

Out in St. Louis, the game is **Cork Ball.** The ball is a ball of cork, 1½ inches in diameter, that is wrapped in layers of electricians' tape to give it size and heft. The pitcher pitches on a fly, and the batter is allowed one swing. If he misses he is out unless the catcher drops the ball, in which case the miss doesn't count.

PEGGY

Yet another baseball-type game is the South Boston game of Peggy, which uses a wooden clothespin (with the knob at the end whittled to a point) for the ball and a venetian blind slat for a bat.

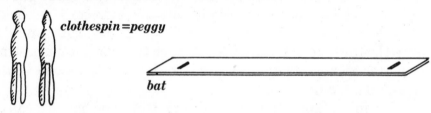

clothespin = peggy

bat

The batter in this rule-laden game holds the bat up with one end on the ground as the pitcher throws the peggy at it. If he hits the bat, the pitcher becomes the batter. If he misses, the batter measures the distance from the bat to where the peggy landed in bat lengths and whatever that comes to becomes part of his run total. For example, if it's four slat lengths away, he has four runs. Then, the batter, using an edge of his bat, strikes down on the whittled point of the peggy, making it flip into the air; and while it is in flight, he hits it with the bat.

If the pitcher catches the peggy, a risky situation if the point is flying at him, he becomes the batter. If not, he again pitches it at the upended bat and the game goes on. This game continues until a player gets the 100 points needed to win.

This game seems to be an adaptation, with baseball runs and the concepts of pitcher and catcher added, of a game called **Cat** which originated in Italy and Germany. In that game, the cat (a small piece of wood) is tossed toward an area marked off or dug into the ground while a defender with a bat smacks it away. And it is akin to the English game of **Stick and Goose,** in which the basic stick is about 6 inches long and about 1½ inches wide and whittled to a point at each end.

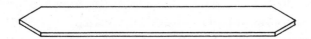

A player strikes the stick at one end with a broomstick, forcing it to flip upward, and then bats away at it. Whoever hits it farthest wins.

PUNCHBALL

Stick and Goose is not that far removed from Stickball, not at all. Even more similar are baseball-type games using a spaldeen and the players' bare hands instead of a bat. The best-known is Punchball, which is exactly like Stickball except that the ball is hit with the fist, palm forward, just as if the hitter is holding a tennis racket in his hand. A well-thumped hit can easily go one and a half sewers, and all the rules governing strikes, outs, and innings are similar to those for Stickball.

Two short-range Punchball games are far more challenging. The first, called **Short Ball,** is played, not along the length of the gutter, but between the sidewalks in a marked-off diamond.

sidewalk

third base
second base
pitcher
home
first base

sidewalk

The ball is pitched to the batter on a bounce, and the hitter has to punch at it, making certain that it bounces once within the playing-field area. If the ball is hit on a fly over any boundary, it is an automatic out. The accent in this game is on fielding.

Even more demanding is **Triangle,** created up in the Crotona section of the Bronx.

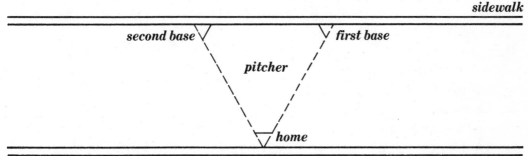

Again, the ball is pitched on a bounce, and the batter has to hit a ground ball that will bounce within the playing area. A ball hit on a fly out of the triangle is an out, and a grounder that peels off foul before reaching a base is a foul. Two fouls and the batter is out.

Because of the confined playing surfaces, both games are also played as versions of **Slap Ball,** which is essentially Punchball except that the ball is hit with the open palm. Slap Ball produces virtually no fly balls, but ground balls are often trickier to handle because a skillful batter can chop downward and skim the spaldeen, putting "English" on the ball as it bounces toward the fielders.

CURB BALL

Of course, if you are all too lazy to draw a playing area, there is always **Curb Ball,** which is essentially Stoopball played where there aren't stoops but where a fine curb, preferably granite, is available. The ball is thrown by hand against the curb, bouncing first on the riser and then on the street or on the point. A base is awarded for each bounce of the spaldeen. As in all these ball games, the rules of baseball apply.

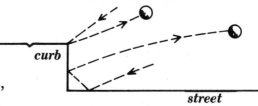

curb

street

A danger that players constantly live with—in addition to the considerable tension that arises when one comes to bat with the bases loaded and then has to wait for a car to pass through the playing field—is that the spaldeen can go down a sewer. It happens often, but there are ways not only of getting it back but also of ensuring that a loss is only transitory. A tomato juice can, punctured on the side to allow a string to be passed through and punctured on the bottom as well to let water in, is lowered into the sewer, submerged, and pulled up under the floating spaldeen. I never saw it fail. On the other hand, when a grouch confiscates a ball, or when it is known that such a possibility exists, the owner yells, "Chips," or "Money chips," before the game begins. Thus, if the spaldeen is lost, the other players are bound to chip in for a new one. A fair arrangement.

ON THE SEWER

Playing in the street taught us all we ever wanted to know about sewers. We knew it was bad to throw discarded cartons down sewers because it made for flooded street corners on rainy days. Sewers were messy, but we never connected them with manholes, the covers of which served us in so many ways. A sewer was dirty, and God forbid if the marbles you were rolling along the gutter next to the curb went too far and dropped through the grating, for your mib was forever lost. So, we were careful of sewers.

The cast-iron manhole covers (whose designs are being collected by architectural historians) were something else again. They were home plate for Stickball and Punchball, second base in other games, pitchers' mounds, kickoff tees for football, free-throw lines for basketball, pedestals for Statues, safe zones in Tag. The way one marbles game is played is dictated by the design of manhole covers. On New York City's East Side, it is called On the Sewer.

Marbles are set on all the raised portions of the geometric designs on the cover (a certain number are contributed by each shooter) and then aimed at and shot off by the players in turn. Marbles knocked off their embossed-iron perches are kept by the player who knocks them off as long as they bounce off the manhole cover and into the street. A fine shooters' game, with the shooting being done by raising one's shooting hand several inches off the ground, making the aiming that much more difficult.

KICK THE CAN

Manhole covers also provided the stage for one of the street games dearest to the hearts of children the world over simply because it makes the most noise: Kick the Can. It is played in different ways, and different games are called by the same name, but the constant is that a manhole cover is an esthetic necessity. A can is not ready for kicking until it is perched in the middle of a manhole cover.

In many parts of the eastern United States, Kick the Can is a baseball-type game, played either in the space defined by street corners or in a diamond drawn on one street, like this:

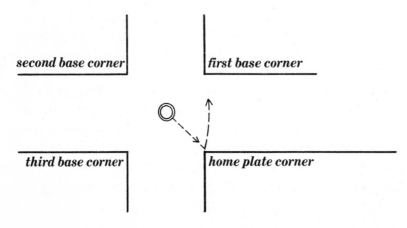

second base corner

first base corner

third base corner

home plate corner

or like this:

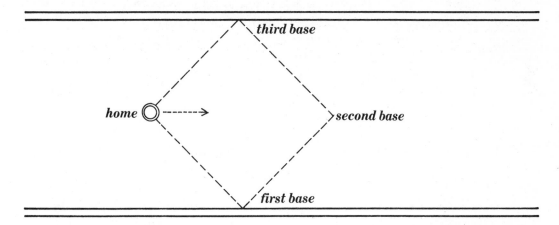

In the four-corner version, the manhole cover is the pitcher's mound; in the drawn-diamond version, it is the batter's box. In both games, it is where the can begins. In the four-corner game, the pitcher rolls the can to the home plate corner, and the batter kicks it. The pitcher then has to catch it (on a fly is an out) or on the ground, pick it up, run to the base, and place it upright on the corner before the batter reaches the base. Otherwise, baseball rules apply, as they do in the drawn-diamond version, in which the batter kicks the can without benefit of a pitcher and runs the bases. The can is used in the same ways as a baseball or a spaldeen.

     The most famous game of Kick the Can, as universal a game as there is, is played this way: One person is "It," chosen by "odd finger." One of the other players, perhaps the one wearing shoes instead of sneakers is the kicker. After a running start, he boots the can as far as he can. Then, as "It" *walks* after the can, all the other players hide. "It" brings the can back to the designated manhole cover, puts his foot on it, and counts to 200 or 300 by fives. He is then free to seek out those hiding. When he sees one, he races back to the can, puts a foot on it, and shouts, "Putty on the can, I see Abe behind the stoop!" Whereupon Abe surrenders, comes back to the manhole cover, and stands "in jail." As soon as "It" captures all the players, the game is over. The first man caught then becomes "It."

However, heartbreak happens when, for example, Abe has captured say five of the six players and, while he is out searching, the sixth races to home base, shouting "All free," and kicks the can clattering down the gutter. "It" then has to begin all over again. A fine game of frustration, totally suited to the streets because there is nothing to match the sound of can clanging against pavement.

RED ROVER

Many games of urban gutters and suburban streets involve getting from one curb to the other. Simple enough. But the variations on the theme and the obstacles presented are many and inventive. The best-known is Red Rover, which in all its versions requires two teams, usually of about six players each; one version also calls for a man in the middle. The two teams range themselves on opposite sides of the street and within chalked-off boundaries. If chalk is in short supply, a telephone pole, a fire hydrant, a parked auto, or somebody's hedge become agreed-upon boundaries.

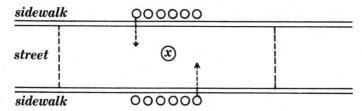

In the simplest version of Red Rover, the man in the middle (chosen by "odd finger") is "It." He stands in the middle of the street and, beginning with one team, points to one member and chants, "Red Rover, Red Rover, let Chrissie come over!" Chrissie then has to dash across the street, remaining within the specified boundaries without being tagged. If Chrissie is tagged, he remains in the center as an assistant to "It."

Then, "It" repeats the process with a member of the team on the opposite side of the street. The winner of the game is the last person on either team to escape being tagged. There is almost never one winner. Two or three of the swiftest players usually last through two or three crossovers, and a standoff is declared.

Another version has the two teams but no middleman. The captain of each team does the chanting: "Red Rover, Red Rover, let Johnny come over!" Johnny takes off toward the chanting team. In this version, all members of the defending team link arms, and it is Johnny's business to try and break through any link that he can. If he succeeds, he is free to return to his own team. If he fails, he becomes part of the team he runs into. The game seesaws back and forth, with the ultimate end being one long line of kids, arms linked, on one sidewalk. This second version, the most common both in this country and in Great Britain, is called **Germany** in some cities.

In addition, there is **Three Steps to Germany,** also called **Three Feet off to Germany,** which is essentially a Red Rover game, but with an interesting fillip. In this game, "It" stands by himself on one sidewalk while a group of players stand on the other. "It" designates who is to run and then shouts, "Go!" The named player has to reach the other sidewalk without being tagged by "It." If he is successful, he returns once again to the other side and runs again. If he fails, he joins "It," linking arms, and the next player called has to run directly at the two and attempt to break through the link. Whoever lasts the longest is the winner.

The basic requirement in this game is the three broad steps that the named player has to take before attempting his dash into the human chain, thus the names Three Steps and Three Feet.

Another game using three steps as the basis for attempting an untagged trip across a street is the Chicago game of **Three Steps Across.** What makes this game interesting is that it is impossible. It is played by three; two are the runners, and the other is "It." The two runners have to step back as far from the edge of their sidewalk as possible, take a running start, and then take the longest three steps possible into the street. The name of the game indicates that a player should be able to get across an average gutter in three long steps, which is possible only I suppose for Kareem Abdul-Jabbar. At the end of the three steps, a runner has to freeze in place, not moving, not toppling over, in whatever position he lands after his third step.

Whoever is "It" then stands and surveys the heavily breathing runner, and if the runner so much as hitches his shoulder, he is tagged and becomes "It." On the other hand, if "It" gives too much attention to one runner, the other can quickly dash to the opposite curb, which makes him safe until he tries the three steps into the street and back across the street.

Another version of Three Steps Across is more tantalizing because the emphasis changes from the possibility of being tagged simply because one is off-balance to agility and the ability to decoy.

Before any player makes the dash across the street, he takes three giant steps from his home curb, in slow motion, which effectively cuts down his dodging range.

GIANT STEPS

Giant Steps as it is known almost everywhere is also called **Steps** in Connecticut and **May I?** in Chicago. This is also a sidewalk-to-sidewalk game across a street. To be "It" is enviable in this game because the object is to stay "It" as long as possible.

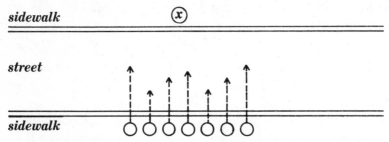

"It" has the option of determining how each player on the opposite sidewalk can move and how far. "It" asks, "Is everybody ready?" When all agree, he says, "Beverly may take two baby steps." Beverly then takes two steps into the street toward the other curb, *but only* after she asks, "May I?" Moving before asking automatically sends the stepper all the way back to where he or she began.

This game is notable for the inventiveness of its steps. "Baby steps" are tiny, mincing steps. "Lady steps" are slightly longer in length (the way kids think ladies walk). "Scissors steps" are taken with legs apart in a jumping motion. "Grasshopper steps" are forward leaps on bent knee. For "barrel steps," you move ahead by spinning around once with each step. "Rabbit steps" are taken by hopping up and down with your feet together. But "giant steps" are the longest-possible strides.

The object of the game is to get precisely to the opposite curb, and it was up to "It" to keep you from doing that by mixing up the steps called. For example, if a player has made an advance to about one stride from the curb, "It" might say to the player, "Take three giant steps," knowing the distance will send him far past the curb. The player then steps off without saying "May I?," figuring it is better to run away and try again. A game of decoying, of "It" knowing that one player's "lady steps" are another's "giants." The first player to touch the curb with a designated series of steps replaces "It." There are, of course, sneaky steps to take surreptiously in the hope that "It" does not see.

Another facet of the game that provides difficulty is the order of steps called out. "It" might say, for example, "Maria may take one giant, two scissors, a rabbit, and a baby." Even if Maria says, "May I?," she still has to perform the right number of steps in the right order or she is sent back.

Those without patience usually stay away from Giant Steps.

UNCLE SAM, UNCLE SAM

Preparation, not patience, is necessary for Uncle Sam, Uncle Sam, which, like other street games, combines guessing, running, and tagging. Again, two sidewalks and the street in between constitute the playing field. Whoever is Uncle Sam stands on one side, and his Nieces and Nephews stand on the other. Uncle Sam stands there, arms crossed, looking solemn while the first player sings, "Uncle Sam, Uncle Sam, may we cross your golden dam?" (For some unaccountable reason, the Bronx version of the chant is, "Uncle Sam, Uncle Sam, may we cross your dirt dam?")

Uncle Sam looks and answers, "Not unless you have the color————;" and he names any color he chooses. If a player has the color either on his back or anywhere in his posession, he is, in one version, allowed to take one step toward Uncle Sam. In this way, he can inch across the street with each correct color he has. In another version, he is permitted safe passage across the street. A player without the color either remains where he is and awaits another turn (in the first version), or tries to dash across the street to the other sidewalk before being tagged (in the second version). One is a slow game; the other, fast. The slow game is preferred by most, particularly those who, expecting to play Uncle Sam, Uncle Sam, take their mothers' thread

206

samplers with them when they go out to play. A wise, winning stratagem.

A similar game is **Red Light, Green Light.** In this game, whoever is "It" stands on one sidewalk while all other players stand on the opposite side. "It" then turns his back to the others, and when he shouts, "Green light," they can run toward him. But they are always brought to screeching halts when he quickly follows with, "Red light," and turns around. Anyone caught moving is sent back across the street to the starting line. The winner is the player who manages, in a series of moves between "Green light" and "Red light," to get close enough to "It" to touch him.

Another version has "It" saying, "Red light, green light, 1, 2, 3," while the others run at him, but this is not as demanding as the other. However, saying, "R-e-d- light, green light 1, 2, 3," in triple time is almost certain to catch a player or two in a misstep.

Also similar is **Mister Fox,** a New Jersey game for three or more players. "It" (Mister Fox) stands on one sidewalk while the other players stand on the other, across the street. The others keep asking him, "What time is it, Mister Fox?" He can answer with any time he chooses (11:29, 4:17, 1:30, 7:38, whatever), but the instant he says, "Twelve noon," all the other players must dash past him if possible to the other curb before he is able to tag them. When one is tagged, he becomes Mister Fox's helper and the two of them become catchers. When all players have been caught, the first one who was tagged by Mister Fox becomes Mister Fox for the next game.

A sidewalk-to-sidewalk game that combines many elements of other games is a San Francisco innovation called **One Foot off the Gutter.** Once again, it begins with the player designated "It" standing on one sidewalk and all other players standing across the street. In this game, "It" is called the Breaker, and he has to race across the street and break through the other players' linked arms anywhere he can. If he fails he goes back and tries again. If he is successful, all members of the human chain have to free themselves quickly and race across to the other sidewalk. The Breaker is the judge of the race, and whomever he deems to have finished last becomes "It".

At this point, the game is much like Tag, with "It" chasing after the others as they run back and forth across the street. Anyone tagged becomes "Its" helper. The winner is the last player left untagged, and he becomes the Breaker for the next game.

There is a great deal of opportunity for roughhouse in this game, particularly when the Breaker busts through, because it is not beneath one player who is arm-linked to another to attempt to throw him back in order to get an advantage in the dash across the street.

STATUES

Another game, an import from England that acquired additional touches as it made its way through the United States is Statues, known also in the eastern part of the country as **Freeze.**

One player is "It" and stands in the gutter just off the curb. All other players line up on the sidewalk with their toes just at the edge of the curb. "It" asks each player in turn, "Do you want salt, pepper, mustard, or vinegar?" Depending upon the answer given he grabs the player's arm and pulls him or her into the street. "Salt" is a moderate pull; "pepper," slightly harder; "mustard," much harder, and vinegar," a socket-stretching yank. As "It" lets go of a player's arm, that player has to remain still and in the position in which he has landed.

Then, "It" decides upon a category (such as farm animals, cowboys, sports, whatever), announces it, and shouts, "Begin!" At this point, all the statues, in position, have to act out as best they can an interpretation of the category. Then, "It" shouts, "Freeze," and all the statues must stay still. "It" then calls, "Lights out," and all the statues close their eyes. "It" now assumes the role of an art critic, passing among the statues and making remarks about their poses and construction, most of them highly uncomplimentary. Anyone laughing (which "It" tries to force) or moving a muscle is eliminated from the game.

Then, "It" tells the remaining statues to open their eyes, and he reveals

Freeze!

which statue he has chosen as the best—a totally subjective opinion. That person becomes "It" for the next game of Statues. There is a disadvantage when "It" and a very good friend are both in the game because favoritism can destroy competition. But most "Its" try their best, like most art critics, to be objective and to consider the statuary on artistic merit only. Don't they?

No, they don't.

A far simpler version, which is also considerably rougher, is **Swinging Statues.** Whoever is "It" simply swings each of the other players around by an arm four times and lets him fly. The players must remain immobile in the positions they land in. Then, he decides which of his creations is best and that statue becomes the swinger. Little sophistication in this version, but an equal opportunity for favoritism.

AGGRESSION

Swinging Statues is an apt introduction to some of the rougher of the games of the gutter. Perhaps *games* is not the word, but they are pastimes and strangely enough are enjoyed hugely by those who partake of them.

One of these is **Poison.** A group of players joins together by placing their arms over and under the shoulders of their neighbors and form a circle. A ball, usually a basketball, is put on a manhole cover, and the circle surrounds it. At a signal, everyone tries to force his neighbor against the ball, hoping to force the neighbor to nudge it, kick it, even fall on it. Whoever ultimately does so is Poison, or "It," and a game of Tag ensues. There are no niceties in this game, no strategy, just force.

Arm wrestles, leg wrestles, hand wrestles, and finger wrestles abound in the street, all contributing to the machismo of the gutter. To most kids, strength is enviable, even though cleverness is pretty good, too. A favorite game, concocted in New York's West Side Chelsea district, in which the anticipation is far greater than the participation is something called **Election Night.** For months preceding the first Tuesday of November each year, youngsters gather scraps of wood. (Lumber is stolen from building sites; tree branches are collected; orange crates are broken up and stacked.) After dark on election night, a suitable street, the busier with auto traffic the better, is selected, and a vast, quarter-block-long bonfire is set. It really is not all that dangerous because it is set in the middle of the street, but the illumination and the crowd of policemen and firemen it draws are most satisfying.

A similar intellectual exercise is **Flour and Ashes,** which requires its players to be agile and to have acceptable bludgeoning technique.

Basic equipment is a discarded or confiscated knee-length woolen sock. It is carefully darned if it has holes in it and then knotted just above the toe. Then, it is stuffed full of either flour or coal-stove ashes. The game is then ready to be played. Players declare themselves members of one team or another, and the teams set out after each other, belting each other with the filled socks.

Nobody really gets hurt in this game, but over whatever gutter is the afternoon's battlefield there rises the densest cloud of white outside of a chemical fire. As soon as a player's sock is empty, he has to retire to the curb and cheer on his friends, waiting to see who will be the best and the whitest.

Another roughhouse game is **Grab the Flag,** in which the flag is a white handkerchief stuck into a player's belt behind his back and left dangling. It is limited to two players, but challengers can stand in line to play the winner. Like wrestlers, the two flag holders circle each other, arms extended, and try quick grabs at the handkerchiefs. Players are allowed to push and shove with their hands, arms, and shoulders, but no kicking.

This, again, is a game for the quick, with much feinting and dodging and position faking. The winner, of course, is the player who succeeds in tearing the handkerchief out of his opponent's belt. Usually, a chalked-off area is created in the street (sort of a macadam wrestling mat), and the players have to remain within the area or forfeit the match. Like most games of its sort, Grab the Flag is the cause of whole series of black-and-blue marks as well as red-welted hickeys up and down the arms.

No discussion of rough gutter games would be complete without some mention of a charming game that was born in New York in 1940, thrived during the years of World War II, nurtured by the war films of Warner Brothers and the specter of Otto Preminger that hung over the repeated torture-questionings of Errol Flynn and Paul Henreid. The game?

Gestapo. Gestapo? Yes, Gestapo.

It involved two teams, who could be RAF flyers downed in occupied France on the run from the Nazis or American saboteurs on the run, either group being pursued relentlessly by the Gestapo. The good guys usually had about a five-minute head start and ran off and hid anywhere in the neighborhood within a two-block radius. Then, the Gestapo would begin searching. When they caught a good guy, they didn't just take him to Jail. It was a requirement of the game that the prisoner be manhandled, perhaps dragged, and that he resist strongly. Jail was anywhere (a stoop, a marked-off square in the street, a patch of sidewalk), and once in, the prisoner's shoes and socks were removed so that he couldn't escape. Then an interrogation was begun to force the prisoner to reveal where the others were hidden.

Involved were such things as placing the prisoner in a fruit crate and hitting the crate with sticks, tickling the balls of his feet until he shreiked for mercy, pulling up his shirt and giving him a "pink belly" (creating a bright red stomach area by constant pat-pat-patting on the stomach), and of course, threatening him with all the tortures that Preminger used to visit upon Flynn.

Oddly enough, most of us who played Gestapo enjoyed our role playing immensely; and the tortures although often hurtful, were not permanently painful. If that makes any sense. Gestapo dropped out of favor after the war.

HOCKEY

What is as rough as any street game, but which has its origins in organized sport, is Hockey, city-gutter style. Equipment is necessary for this game, so nets are constructed from discarded crates, hockey sticks are made by taping the cut-off corner of an orange crate to the end of a broomstick, and rolls of black electricians' tape become pucks.

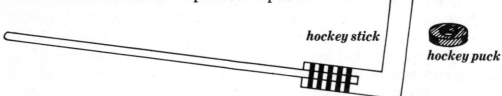

hockey stick

hockey puck

There are no such things as blue lines or center ice or things like that. One team on roller skates simply tries to send the roll of tape into the other team's net while that team tries to stop them. There is some cross-the-street passing, some passable stickhandling, quite a few shots taken by both teams, but all this is secondary to the mayhem that playing the game sanctions. Body checks send players zooming off-balance over curbs and falling heavily on their rumps, and blows from the makeshift sticks abound. Needless to say, the team with the most goals wins. Often, it is a case of one team having more men on the field simply because there are more survivors. Definitely a hickey game—and more so.

TOUCH FOOTBALL

Roughness also prevails with the two versions of football spawned on the streets: **Touch Tackle** and **Association.** The games are virtually identical except that it is understood that if there are more than two players to a side, the game is Touch Tackle, not Association. Both games are truncated football, but Association, with its smaller teams, is faster moving.

On a street, the football field usually spans two telephone poles; if the passers are exceptional, this is extended to three telephone poles. No kicking is permitted. Instead, when a team kicks off, the best passer throws the ball as far as he can. The other team can run and pass the ball back in any combination it chooses, and no play is considered over until either a player holding the football is tagged by a member of the opposing team or a pass is dropped.

In Association, only one down is permitted, so virtually every play is a long "go out as far as you can and I'll get the ball to you" pass play. Often, if only three players are available, the best passer on the block remains the steady passer for both teams. A fast, shifty runner can run for a touchdown, or virtually assure his team of one if he eludes the defender who is guarding him. The runner then races downfield, and the player on the other team defending against the pass is forced to come up to try and stop him, whereupon a little looping pass is thrown to the receiver. Touchdown—6 points!

The roughness of the game is in the "touch." Rules agreed upon before

It's not the NFL, but it's just as tough.

the first kickoff decide the tenor of the play. "One-hand touch" is not too bad. But there are games played with "slap touch" and "two-hand touch," and these are violent indeed. A heavy-handed slap on a player's back as he is running is quite painful, and "two-hand touches" are more often two-handed shoves that send ballcarriers and passers sprawling headlong onto the concrete.

With Touch Tackle, the game assumes more of the elements of football. Teams range in size from six to a full complement of eleven. Blocking is permitted both at the line of scrimmage after the ball is snapped and downfield. Players are also permitted to use their hands to fend off blocking, and many downs degenerate into all-out fistfights. Each side is permitted downs. Consequently, different strategies are available, including of course the all-or-nothing long pass. In most Touch games, the touch is two-handed, so that along with the blocking and hand offense and defense, there is maximum bodily contact on virtually every play.

As far as boys are concerned, neither Touch Tackle nor Association is a girls' game, although many girls play and are quite good. But generally most boys feel that girls really aren't as bent on hurting people simply for the hell of it, as most of them seem to be.

JUMP ROPE

Just as boys chauvinistically expect girls to stay away from the rough-housing that they regarded as their special province, girls regard Jump Rope as an activity that boys really aren't interested in. And just as surely as the boys' assumption is not totally true, neither is the girls'. I can remember playing Jump Rope, enjoying it immensely, and coming back for more.

Jump Rope, single rope (which I remember we called just **Ropes),** is relatively easy to join in on once you get the rhythm ticking properly in your head and then time the jump into the turning rope with precision. More difficult is **Double Dutch,** in which a double length of clothesline is used, with one turner, or Ender, wrapping it behind her back, over her forearms, and through her hands while the other Ender holds the two ends. You can also play with two ropes. In Double Dutch, great stress is placed on the Ender to prevent the rope from "kissing" (slapping together) and thus ruining the flow of the jumps and the rhymes that Jump Rope is filled with. For the ordinary jumper, the ropes are turned slowly; but for those who are known as terrific jumpers, the Enders deliver "mustard and pepper," a speeded-up turning that tests jumping powers greatly.

Of course, at least three players are needed—two to turn, one to jump—although fastening one end of rope to a fence or around a fire hydrant will do in a pinch. The gutter is ideal for Jump Rope, particularly for Double Dutch, in which the ropes go out in long, looping arcs.

The skill of Jump Rope involves entering the turning length of rope, jumping precisely to whatever rhythm the Enders have established, then jumping out exactly at the right time, too, either to complete the rhyme or to permit another jumper into the rope. The inventiveness of the game of Jump Rope or Ropes lies in the rhymes.

The simpler Jump Rope rhymes begin with some doggerel that then leads into counting because it is the counting that denotes one's staying power in the rudimentary jump rope games. Here are several:

Napoleon with his bones apart,
He tried to save his France.
He crossed the Channel, and he fought,
But they kicked him in the pants.
They kicked him, they kicked him.
How often did they kick him?
One time, two times, three times

Teacher, teacher with the bamboo stick,
Wonder what I got in arithmetic?
Ten, twenty, thirty, forty

Fire, fire, false alarm
Irving fell in Brigitte's arms.
How many kisses did he receive?
Close your eyes, and you will see.
One, two, three, four, five

Double Dutch requires nimble feet . . .

Fudge, fudge, call the judge.
Mama had a newborn baby.
Wrap it up in tissue paper,
Send it down the elevator.
How many hours did baby sleep?
One, two, three, four, five, six

Others use the alphabet, and jumpers or Enders are supposed to make up names such as Zelda Zutts, so that the jumper will have to go through the alphabet twice to get to the first name and then the last name of her sweetheart. The rhyme is:

Strawberry shortcake, cream on top,
Tell me the name of your sweetheart.
A, B, C, D, E, F

Other jumping rhymes are just rhymes to be chanted by each jumper, after which she jumps out of the turning rope and another jumper comes in and does the same. Here are two of these:

My mother and your mother
Live across the way.
Every night they have a fight,
And this is what they say.
Acka backa soda cracker,
Acka backa boo.
Acka backa soda craker,
Out goes you.

Teddy bear, teddy bear
Turn around.
Teddy bear, teddy bear
Touch the ground.
Teddy bear, teddy bear
Show your shoe.
Teddy bear, teddy bear
How are you?

Other Jump Rope rhymes have many verses. Here is an example of one that is a Bensonhurst, Brooklyn, favorite:

One, two, three a-leary,
I spy Mrs. Seary
Sitting on a bumble-eary
Just like a little fairy.

One, two three a-light,
I spy Pearl White
Sitting on a golden horse
Knitting for the Red Cross.

Old man Daisy
Thought his wife was crazy.
Up the ladder, down the ladder
Old man Daisy.

House to let.
Inquire within.
Two old ladies drinking gin.
When I get out,
Let Elena come in.

At that point, the next jumper has to jump right in, without missing a beat, as the Enders keep on turning. Many players are poor jumpers and prefer to be turners ("steady Enders") and jumpers are forever in their debt.

When there are many jumpers, games and rhymes designed to provide a continuous flow through the moving ropes are desirable. Such a one is:

On the mountain stands a lady.
Who she is I do not know.
All she wants is gold and silver.
All she wants is a nice young man.
So jump in, my Grace,
And jump out, my Tess.

Tess is the jumper who jumps out, as Grace jumps in and repeats the rhyme, calling in the next jumper on line.

By all accounts, the most famous of all Jump Rope rhymes is "Cinderella," which is known in various versions all over the world. Watch any bunch of children jumping rope, and sometime before the session is over, you'll hear:

Cinderella dressed in yella
Went downtown to see her fella.

On the way her panties busted.
How many people were disgusted?
One, two, three, four

Cinderella dressed in yella
Went downstairs to the kitchen sink.
The kitchen sink was full of ink.
How many mouthfuls did she drink?

Cinderella dressed in yella
Went out dancing with her fella.
On the way her petticoat busted.
This is how many were disgusted.

Cinderella dressed in yella
Went upstairs to kiss a fella.
How many kisses did she give?
One, two, three, four

Each jumper goes into the rope (single or Double Dutch) for one stanza and stays jumping, counting as high as she wants or jumping out after an agreed-upon number (say, fifty), and then the next jumper comes in. The rhymes in "Cinderella" are often made up on the spot. And even if the rhymes barely rhyme, so what. Ropes is the thing.

...and everlasting breath.

PUSSY IN THE CORNER

Often in street games, *doing* is as much fun as *preparing*—laying out impromptu rules for impromptu games, choosing for "firsties," electing captains, planning strategies, creating playing fields with chalk. These can be as simple or as intricate as the rules of the game decided upon dictate.

A simple field for a simple game is in order for Pussy in the Corner. Two curbs form two boundaries, two chalk lines, the other boundaries; and a manhole cover is where "It" stands.

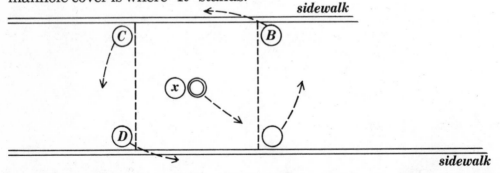

"It" stands in the middle, and one player stands at each corner of the field. At a signal given by one of them (either meowing like a cat, purring, or

saying softly, "Here, pussy. Here, pussy."), the players move coun-
terclockwise to the next corner. It is up to "It" to reach any corner left open
before the next player gets to it. Which is not as easy as it sounds because the
signal can be false and accompanied by a feinting move, causing "It" to jump
one way while the action begins behind him. However, if "It" gets to a corner
first, the player without a corner goes to the manhole and becomes the Pussy
in the middle.

STREET POOL

Just as simple is the diagram for Street Pool, a game in which the gutter, or at least a small piece of it, becomes sort of a billiard table.

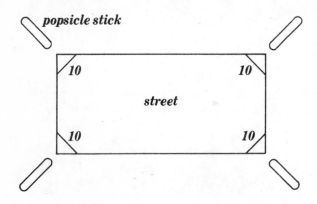

A popsicle stick is placed at each corner of the playing area, directly at the point and touching it. Players take turns trying to flip the sticks (using other popsicle sticks) into the corner areas, which are worth 10 points each. If the stick goes beyond the corner into the box or backward away from the corner, no points are scored and the player loses his turn. A landing in a 10 corner gives 10 points and a chance to go again. The winning socre is 100 points. Sort of a tiddledywinks of the street, was Street Pool.

STREET CHECKERS

Street Checkers has three versions—small, bigger, and biggest—the size of the checkerboard depending on the size of the checkers. A simple rectangle is chalked off in the street, and a stake of regular checkers (perhaps as many as five per player) is set inside the rectangle. Then, the shooters shoot them out, marbles style, with shooters that are other checkers (small game), a smoothly sanded wooden disk about 2½ inches in diameter (bigger game), and a roll of black electricians' tape (biggest game), which also serves as a Hockey puck. The shooter is placed flat on the ground shot by flicking the forefinger off the thumb and hitting it straight on.

This is a "for keeps" game, and a player having a good day can earn himself a complete set of blacks and reds for in-the-house checkers.

SKELLY

Skelly, surely the quintessential New York City street game, uses checkers—bottle caps filled with wax for weight, glass bottle tops worn smooth, brick chips, and the caps from half-gallon wine jugs as shooters—and are shot just as in **Street Checkers.**

The only similarities between Street Checkers and Skelly is in the checkers and the finger-shooting position. There the resemblance ends. Skelly, also known as **Skelsy, Scully Pit, Tops,** and **Caps,** appears to be native to and confined to New York City. It utilizes skill, strategy, luck, vengeance, and nastiness and is a most entertaining way to spend an afternoon—for Skelly is one of those games that, like Monopoly, goes on interminably. The diagram is complex:

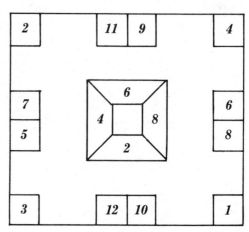

Skelly, Skelsy, Tops, Caps—is the name important?

The object of the game is to go from box 1 to box 13 (in the progression 1, 2, 3, 4, 5, and so on), then return the same way from 13 to 1, then go back to 13 again, and then back again to 1, after which you become a Killer. And when a Killer hits another player, that player is out of the game. All shots have to be taken by shooting the forefinger off the thumb, as in Street Checkers. Sounds simple and direct, right?

Wrong.

The object of the game is not only to move yourself through the course four times but also to prevent all your opponents from doing likewise. So, if you find yourself next to another's bottle cap, instead of shooting for the next square, you can shoot him as far off the Skelly field as possible so that he has to start from square 1 again. In some versions of the game, this entitles you to go automatically to the next square for which you are headed; other versions permit you an extra shot toward your next box. Sending an opponent ten or twenty feet down the gutter is called "messing him up" and is almost as exhilarating as going through the course completely.

When shooting into the numbered boxes, no "linies" (shots resting on the line) are permitted. The shooter has to be all the way in the numbered box.

Getting to the 13 box carries with it much danger. In some versions, the four areas around the 13 box (called "skels") have number values. If you land in any of them, you are forced to stay there for as long as the other players want you to. The only way you can leave is if another player shoots you out. This, however, entitles that player to the number of boxes indicated by the number of the skel. Thus, if you have gone through 12 and, in shooting for 13, land in the skel valued at 8, another player who is only at 5 can hit you out and automatically go into 13, which is the total of the number of boxes he had already moved through and the penalty value of the skel.

In other versions, the skels have no numbered values and look like this:

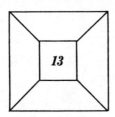

In this case, the player in the skel is still obliged to remain there until another player knocks him out, but the rewards are not so great. The hitter, is awarded either another shot or the next square. But in the unnumbered-skels version, an added feature is the requirement that a player go through each skel, one at a time, en route from box 12 to box 13. So, if you have been into 12, you must go into each skel at least once before you can go into 13.

However, it is a fact that players *do* get through the course four times and *do* become Killers. And in what is there more joy than in drawing a bead on a fellow player—perhaps one who has tortuously made his way through three courses and is on his way through the fourth—and knocking him down the street and out of the game?

Joy. Joy in the streets!

ALLEYS A consideration

Flea
Fly
Flea, fly, flow
Coomalana coomalana veesta.
Oh, no
No, not the veesta veesta.
Eeny meeny desameeny
Oo ah awalameeny.
Beep diddly oten doten
Bobo but deeten dotten.

THERE ARE A few games that do not lend themselves to the geometrics of sidewalk squares, to stoops and empty lots, or to the tarry expanses of the gutter for the very good reason that they were conceived in and for the narrow confines of alleys.

Now, some people confuse driveways with alleys. There are a lot of driveways around these days; cars use them to get to garages. But there are fewer and fewer alleys. Alleys are usually found between two many-story buildings but can also be narrow concrete strips between the backyards of rows of houses on adjacent streets. They are marvelous echo chambers and have built-in boundaries and limitations—called walls—that effectively do away with fair-or-foul arguments. They are more private than streets and are often ignored, but they cannot be overlooked here simply because most streets lead into alleys and sometimes street game trickle into alleys.

A wonderful alley game called **Wire Ball** involves throwing a spaldeen against the triple strands of telephone wires that span every alley ever made. The object of the game is to throw the ball into the wires, skimming through them, so that it travels on through and is not caught by the player standing underneath the wires. With a football, you can punt through the wires. Nice, nice.

Softball, alley style, carries rigid rules. A soft ball hit off the wires and caught is an out. A ball that hits or even grazes a house wall and is caught before hitting the ground is an out. A ball that lands atop any shed, house, or garage roof is an out. So is a ball landing in any yard.

And what was safe, you ask? Any line drive to dead center (straight down the alley), so long as it isn't caught. Pull hitters shun alley Softball.

236

There are alley versions of Handball, Punchball, and Stickball, but they really don't work out too well. But what is really good in alleys are tin cans to which string is attached and stretched across the alley from one window to another window in another house. They are free telephones. Where else can you get free phone service today?

INDEX OF GAMES